CLOWNFISH IN GAMING

Clownfish in Gaming

From Virtual Oceans to Playful Pixels

OLIVIA K.

Spectra Enterprise

Contents

INDEX

INTRODUCTION

In the immense span of the computerized domain, where imagination combines with innovation, a far-fetched at this point captivating hero has tracked down its place - the clownfish. Starting from the energetic coral reefs of this present reality, these notable marine animals have risen above their normal living space to become virtual natives of gaming scenes. This investigation digs into the dazzling excursion of clownfish in gaming, exploring the development from sensible portrayals in virtual seas to charming portrayals in perky pixels.

1. The Starting points of Gaming and Virtual Domains
   To comprehend the job of clownfish in gaming, we set out on an excursion through the starting points of the gaming business and the development of virtual domains. From the pixelated scenes of early computer games to the vivid conditions of contemporary augmented simulation, the development of gaming innovation has prepared for the joining of marine life, including the alluring clownfish, into the intelligent texture of advanced universes.
2. Clownfish in reality: Science and Conduct
   Prior to wandering into the virtual area, it is fundamental to disentangle the secrets of clownfish in reality. Investigating their science, conduct, and cooperative associations with ocean anemones gives an establishment to understanding how these enamoring animals have caught the creative mind of both sea life researcher and game planners. From the complicated dance of their dynamic tones to their exceptional conceptive systems, this present reality appeal of clownfish fills in as a rich range for computerized translation.
3. The Rise of Virtual Conditions
   The rise of virtual conditions in gaming addresses a change in

outlook by they way we cooperate with computerized spaces. From the beginning of 2D side-looking over experiences to the three-layered breadths of open-world games, the development of virtual conditions has reflected innovative headways. This segment investigates the achievements that have molded the virtual scenes where clownfish now skip around, from the pixelated oceans to the complicatedly definite submerged domains of present day gaming.

4. **Clownfish as Characters and Buddies**

   In the change from genuine biological systems to virtual conditions, clownfish play expected different parts - from supporting characters to player associates.

   Their presence in gaming goes past simple tasteful allure, impacting interactivity mechanics, account elements, and, surprisingly, profound associations with players. This part disentangles the complex jobs that clownfish play in virtual accounts, analyzing their importance in improving the gaming experience.

5. **Clownfish as Playable Characters: Exploring Advanced Reefs**

   The advancement of gaming has presented to players the extraordinary chance to occupy the computerized shoes, or blades, of different characters. Clownfish, with their unmistakable attributes and ways of behaving, have arisen as playable heroes in specific gaming encounters. This part plunges into the ongoing interaction mechanics, challenges, and narrating subtleties that show some signs of life when players explore virtual reefs as clownfish, opening another element of intuitive narrating.

6. **Nemo's Heritage: Clownfish in Virtual Seas**

   The social effect of clownfish stretches out past the bounds of gaming, owing a lot to the impact of media and film. The worldwide peculiarity lighted by energized characters like Nemo has made a permanent imprint on mainstream society, affecting discernments and igniting interest in marine life. This segment investigates the tradition of clownfish in virtual seas, following the far reaching influences of their advanced portrayals on open mindfulness and protection endeavors.

7. **Prologue to Virtual Seas in Gaming**

   As the virtual seas become more multifaceted and far reaching, an inside and out investigation is justified. This segment fills in as a door to the hypnotizing domains created by game fashioners, where clownfish explore close by a variety of marine life. From the clamoring coral urban areas to the secretive profundities where virtual undertakings unfurl, we dig into the plan methods of reasoning and specialized advancements that reinvigorate these computerized seascapes.

8. **Impact of Marine Life in Game Plan**

The impact of marine life, led by the always well known clownfish, reaches out past simple feel in game plan. From forming level plans to rousing journey stories, the complexities of marine environments assume a urgent part in making vivid gaming encounters. This segment inspects how the regular ways of behaving, connections, and environmental elements of clownfish and other marine species add to the plan rules that oversee virtual submerged universes.

9. **Authenticity in Portraying Clownfish Conduct**

As innovation progresses, the journey for authenticity in portraying clownfish conduct turns into a main impetus in game turn of events. The test lies in truly recreating the nuanced developments, social designs, and cooperative connections saw in the regular world. This segment investigates the undertakings of game engineers to accomplish a degree of loyalty that spellbinds players outwardly as well as instructs them about the complexities of sea life science.

10. **Gaming Advances and Clownfish Authenticity**

The marriage of gaming advances and clownfish authenticity is an entrancing convergence where imaginative inventiveness meets specialized development. From cutting edge illustrations delivering to man-made reasoning reenacting exact ways of behaving, this part analyzes the mechanical headways that add to the uplifted authenticity of clownfish in gaming. The quest for genuineness turns into a demonstration of the steadily developing capacities of gaming innovations.

11. **Close to home Associations with Virtual Marine Life**

Past the visual scene and specialized accomplishments, the close to home reverberation of clownfish in gaming is a demonstration of the force of intelligent narrating. This segment investigates how game architects influence account methods, sound plan, and player associations to manufacture close to home associations among players and virtual marine life. The bond shaped with computerized clownfish rises above pixels, inspiring sympathy and a feeling of stewardship for the seas.

12. **Protection and Instruction through Gaming**

The vivid idea of gaming gives an extraordinary chance to mix diversion instruction and protection. This segment dives into the drives where clownfish and virtual seas act as instructive devices, encouraging mindfulness about marine environments and the difficulties they face. From in-game instructive modules to coordinated efforts with marine preservation associations, gaming turns into a conductor for true effect.

13. **Difficulties and Discussions**

In the journey to coordinate clownfish into gaming scenes, creators and designers experience difficulties and explore expected debates. Offsetting inventiveness with logical precision, tending to moral worries, and accommodating creative freedoms with the safeguarding of marine life become fundamental. This segment investigates the sensitive tightrope stroll between creative articulation and capable portrayal, revealing insight into the difficulties that emerge when lively pixels meet certifiable protection.

14. **Moral Worries in Portraying Marine Life in Games**

Moral contemplations structure the moral spine of gaming improvement, particularly when it includes the portrayal of certifiable environments. This part takes apart the moral difficulties game planners face in depicting marine life, including clownfish, and the obligation they hold in forming public discernments. Finding some kind of harmony between imaginative articulation and protection morals becomes basic for the business' maintainable development.

15. **Effect of Gaming on Certifiable Protection**

The effect of gaming on genuine preservation endeavors turns into a urgent topic as we investigate the potential expanding influences of virtual seas and lively pixels. This segment looks at how gaming encounters including clownfish can move players to draw in with protection drives, support marine exploration, and add to the conservation of coral reefs. The cooperative connection among gaming and protection arises as a strong power for positive change.

16. **Instructive Worth of Virtual Marine Conditions**

Instructive worth lies at the core of the virtual marine conditions where clownfish skip around. This segment dives into the instructive capability of gaming, investigating how virtual seas become dynamic study halls that encourage a comprehension of sea life science, environment, and preservation. From intuitive examples to experiential picking up, gaming turns into an impetus for sustaining the interest and information on players, rising above the limits of customary training.

17. **Associations between Gaming Industry and Preservation Endeavors**

Coordinated effort turns into a foundation in the crossing point of gaming and protection. This segment disentangles the associations manufactured between the gaming business and preservation associations, displaying how joint endeavors enhance the effect of drives focused on marine security. The common objective of encouraging ecological mindfulness and supportability highlights the capability of these coordinated efforts to drive positive change on a worldwide scale.

18. **Difficulties and Contentions: The Tightrope Walk**

The combination of clownfish into gaming scenes brings up basic issues encompassing the moral contemplations, social responsiveness, and potential discussions that arise. This part basically looks at the difficulties looked by the gaming business in exploring these perplexing issues, revealing insight into the fragile equilibrium expected to guarantee that gaming stays a power for good in the domains of schooling and preservation.

19. **Past Clownfish: Investigating Other Marine Life in Gaming**

While clownfish become the overwhelming focus, the more extensive investigation of marine life in gaming divulges a rich embroidery of potential outcomes. This part extends the account to incorporate other marine species, inspecting how their consideration upgrades the variety of virtual environments. From glorious ocean turtles to slippery seahorses, the computerized portrayal of marine biodiversity turns into a demonstration of the gaming business' capability to encourage appreciation for the lavishness of our seas.

20. **Future Prospects and Developments**

As we close this far reaching investigation, the skyline entices with future prospects and developments in the convergence of clownfish, gaming, and marine preservation. This part imagines the direction of gaming encounters, expecting innovative headways, cooperative endeavors, and instructive drives that hold the commitment of molding a manageable and vivid future for virtual seas.

1. Overview of Clownfish

In the complex embroidery of marine life, barely any animals enthrall the creative mind and appeal devotees as much as the clownfish. This outline digs into the interesting universe of these dynamic fish, investigating their science, conduct, natural importance, and the cooperative connections that characterize their reality. From the coral reefs of the Indo-Pacific to the notorious symbolism promoted by vivified films, the clownfish's process unfurls as a demonstration of nature's resourcefulness and the sensitive equilibrium that supports life in the maritime domain.

1. **Scientific categorization and Arrangement**
   The clownfish, having a place with the family Pomacentridae, includes a different gathering of animal types described by their energetic varieties, extraordinary examples, and unmistakable markings. Inside this family, the subfamily Amphiprioninae incorporates the notorious clownfish species, generally known as anemonefish. While there are around 30 perceived species, the most notable among them incorporate the Amphiprion percula, Amphiprion ocellaris, and Amphiprion clarkii.

2. **Geographic Dissemination**
   Clownfish are fundamentally tracked down in the warm waters of the Indo-Pacific district, spreading over from the Red Ocean and the Indian Sea toward the western and focal Pacific Sea. Their appropriation is intently attached to the presence of coral reefs, as these environments give the best natural surroundings to the many-sided ways of life and methods for surviving of clownfish.

3. **Actual Qualities**
   Clownfish are famous for their striking appearance, described by strong hue and unmistakable markings. Normally little in size, going from 2 to 5 crawls long, their bodies show dynamic shades of orange, red, yellow, or dark, frequently decorated with differentiating stripes or examples. These viewable signals fill stylish needs as well as assume a pivotal part in animal categories acknowledgment and correspondence inside their gatherings.

4. **Cooperative Associations with Ocean Anemones**
   One of the most interesting parts of clownfish science is their one of a kind relationship with ocean anemones. In spite of the powerful stinging limbs of these marine spineless creatures, clownfish show a momentous resistance, permitting them to look for shelter among the arms without hurt. As a trade-off for insurance from likely hunters, the clownfish offer the ocean anemones food scraps and hinder parasites. This harmonious bond is an exemplary illustration of mutualism, where the two species benefit from the affiliation.

5. **Social Construction and Regenerative Methodologies**
   Clownfish are known for their mind boggling social designs, frequently shaping gatherings inside the defensive hug of their picked ocean anemones. Each gathering normally comprises of a predominant reproducing pair and a few non-rearing people. The various leveled structure guarantees the regenerative progress of the predominant pair, as they are the sole raisers inside the gathering. Without a trace of the prevailing female, the biggest male goes through a

sex change and expects the reproducing job, featuring the flexibility and strength of clownfish populaces.

6. **Taking care of Propensities and Diet**
Clownfish display omnivorous taking care of propensities, consuming a changed eating routine that incorporates green growth, zooplankton, little shellfish, and debris. Their eating routine may likewise incorporate little spineless creatures possessing their ocean anemone homes. The one of a kind taking care of propensities for clownfish add to the supplement cycling inside coral reef biological systems, highlighting their natural significance in keeping up with the wellbeing of these delicate conditions.

7. **Clownfish and Coral Reefs: Biological Importance**
The presence of clownfish is unpredictably woven into the texture of coral reef environments, adding to their wellbeing and working. By making a mutualistic relationship with ocean anemones, clownfish assume a part in the general biodiversity and solidness of coral reefs. Their exercises, including the expulsion of parasites and air circulation of ocean anemone limbs, add to the prosperity of both the clownfish and their host anemones.

8. **Dangers and Protection Status**
While clownfish have adjusted to life in coral reefs, they face various dangers that risk their populaces. Environmental change-actuated coral blanching, natural surroundings corruption, overcollection for the aquarium exchange, and contamination are critical difficulties. Preservation endeavors mean to address these dangers, zeroing in on environment security, manageable practices in the aquarium exchange, and worldwide drives to battle environmental change and coral reef corruption.

9. **Clownfish in Mainstream society**
The charming appeal of clownfish has not been restricted to the domains of sea life science alone. Their depiction in mainstream society, quite in energized films like "Tracking down Nemo," has raised their status to that of social symbols. This part investigates the impact of clownfish in writing, craftsmanship, and media, analyzing how their portrayal has formed public discernments and added to the more extensive talk on marine preservation.

10. **Research and Logical Commitments**
Clownfish have been subjects of broad logical exploration, contributing important bits of knowledge into sea life science, conduct, and cooperative connections. Analysts have investigated angles, for example, correspondence inside clownfish gatherings, the components of their invulnerability to the ocean anemone poisons, and the

ramifications of their special conceptive methodologies. This segment features key discoveries and the continuous logical undertakings pointed toward disentangling the secrets of clownfish science.

11. Aquarium Keeping and Mindful Proprietorship

The prevalence of clownfish in the aquarium exchange has prompted expanded interest in keeping them as pets. This part underlines the significance of dependable possession, giving experiences into the appropriate consideration, tank prerequisites, and moral contemplations related with keeping clownfish in bondage. Rules for economical practices inside the aquarium exchange are investigated to guarantee the prosperity of these enthralling marine animals.

12. Future Possibilities and Exploration Roads

As how we might interpret clownfish keeps on advancing, future exploration roads hold the commitment of revealing considerably more about these confounding animals.

Progresses in innovation, including hereditary examinations, social perceptions, and natural displaying, offer energizing opportunities for extending our insight into clownfish and their part in marine biological systems. This part guesses on the possible headings of future exploration and the commitments it could make to sea life science.

B. Evolution of Gaming and its Connection to Marine Life

The development of gaming is a dazzling excursion that mirrors headways in innovation, imagination, and the human longing for vivid encounters. As gaming has advanced from straightforward 2D scenes to complex virtual universes, an interesting association has arisen - the joining of marine life into computerized domains. This investigation digs into the harmonious connection between the development of gaming and the portrayal of marine life, looking at what the two have meant for one another and encouraged a one of a kind crossing point where virtual seas wake up with the marvels of the profound.

1. The Beginning of Gaming: From Pong to Pixels

The beginning of gaming can be followed back to the beginning of arcade diversion, where games like Pong denoted the introduction of an industry. As innovation progressed, so did the intricacy of games. The change from pixelated characters to additional itemized sprites and foundations set up for the portrayal of assorted conditions, including submerged scenes. The development of amphibian settings established the groundwork for the consideration of marine life in gaming accounts.

2. **Ascent of Authenticity: Designs, Sound, and Submersion**
   Headways in illustrations and sound advancements play had a significant impact in the development of gaming authenticity. As designers tackled the force of new equipment, the portrayal of marine life progressed from essential sprites to complicated, exact portrayals. Authenticity turned into a sign of gaming encounters, with submerged conditions highlighting schools of fish, coral reefs, and, definitely, notorious marine species like clownfish. The marriage of visual and hear-able authenticity added to vivid gaming, where players felt moved to the profundities of virtual seas.

3. **Investigation and Experience: Submerged Gaming Conditions**
   The development of gaming likewise prompted a change in story center, with investigation and experience becoming focal subjects. Submerged gaming conditions became immense, strange scenes overflowing with marine life. Games like "Perpetual Sea" and "Abzu" exemplified this pattern, permitting players to lower themselves in the magnificence and peril of virtual seas. The portrayal of marine environments became a scenery as well as a necessary piece of the gaming experience.

4. **Innovative Achievements: From 2D to Augmented Reality**
   Mechanical achievements moved gaming into new aspects, in a real sense and metaphorically. The shift from 2D to 3D illustrations opened up opportunities for more complicated marine life portrayals, with species displaying normal ways of behaving and associations. Computer generated reality (VR) made this a stride further, offering players exceptional submersion in submerged universes. Games like "Sea Plummet VR" and "Subnautica" permitted players to investigate the profundities in a genuinely vivid way, enhancing the association among gaming and marine life.

5. **Instructive Gaming: Combining Amusement and Learning**
   The development of gaming has engaged as well as instructed. Instructive gaming encounters have utilized the appeal of marine life to show players sea life science, biological systems, and protection. "Past Blue," for instance, consolidates account driven interactivity with true data about marine life and natural issues. This convergence of diversion and schooling tackles the connecting with nature of gaming to ingrain a feeling of obligation and mindfulness in regards to marine environments.

6. **Impact of Sea life Science: Realness in Gaming**
   As gaming embraced more practical portrayals of marine life, the impact of sea life science turned out to be progressively obvious. Designers looked for interview from sea life scholars to guarantee

exact portrayals of species, ways of behaving, and environments. This joint effort between the gaming business and sea life science added to a more real depiction of submerged conditions. From the development examples of fish to the multifaceted subtleties of coral arrangements, gaming started to mirror the accuracy of sea life science.

7. Notorious Marine Species: Clownfish and Then some

Certain marine species accomplished notorious status in gaming, with the clownfish driving the charge. The ubiquity of clownfish took off, thanks to a limited extent to films like "Tracking down Nemo," and game engineers benefited from their lively varieties and remarkable ways of behaving. Past clownfish, other famous marine species, like dolphins, sharks, and ocean turtles, tracked down their place in gaming stories. These species became characters in virtual seas as well as images of the variety and magnificence of marine life.

8. Narrating and Account Effect: From Nautical Undertakings to Protection Sagas

The advancement of gaming accounts has embraced the huge narrating possible intrinsic in marine conditions. From nautical undertakings and investigation missions to incredible stories of preservation and natural stewardship, gaming has turned into a strong mechanism for passing on messages about marine life.

The story influence stretches out past diversion, affecting players to see the value in the significance of sea protection and the sensitive equilibrium of marine biological systems.

9. Gaming as a Preservation Device: Bringing issues to light and Subsidizing

The association among gaming and marine life has stretched out past virtual domains to genuine preservation endeavors. Games with protection subjects, for example, "Past Blue" and "Unending Sea," intend to bring issues to light about marine issues. Also, gaming stages and engineers have started joint efforts with marine preservation associations, utilizing the gaming local area's scope and monetary help for marine protection drives.

10. Moral Contemplations: Adjusting Diversion and Protection

As the portrayal of marine life in gaming turns out to be more modern, moral contemplations come to the very front. Finding some kind of harmony between diversion worth and protection morals represents a test. Designers should explore issues, for example, overfishing, territory obliteration, and the expected effect of gaming on genuine biological systems. This segment investigates the moral scene of gaming, accentuating the obligation of the business in depicting marine existence with care and thought.

11. **Difficulties and Debates: Exploring Cloudy Waters**
The development of gaming and its association with marine life has not been without difficulties and contentions. From banters about the precision of marine portrayals to worries about the effect of gaming on players' impression of genuine biological systems, the business faces complex issues. Exploring these dim waters requires a nuanced approach that regards both the creative liberty of game designers and the requirement for mindful portrayal of marine life.

12. **The Future Skyline: Developments and Coordinated efforts**

Looking toward the future, the skyline of gaming and its association with marine life is loaded up with conceivable outcomes. Mechanical developments, including increased reality (AR), man-made brainpower (computer based intelligence), and cooperative endeavors between the gaming business and sea life researchers, hold the possibility to rethink the connection among players and virtual seas. This segment hypothesizes on the future bearings of gaming, imagining a scene where the association with marine life turns out to be considerably more significant and effective.

C. Purpose of the Book

The motivation behind the book, "Clownfish in Gaming: From Virtual Seas to Lively Pixels," reaches out past a simple investigation of the computerized portrayal of marine life. It looks to unwind the mind boggling embroidered artwork that entwines gaming, sea life science, and preservation. This try expects to act as a far reaching guide, revealing insight into the multi-layered jobs that clownfish play in the gaming scene while diving into the more extensive ramifications for sea life science, ecological mindfulness, and the developing connection between virtual domains and this present reality.

1. **Revealing the Puzzling Universe of Clownfish in Gaming**
At the center of the book lies the expectation to disclose the mysterious universe of clownfish inside the gaming circle. Perusers leave on an excursion through the development of gaming innovation, from the pixelated expanses of early computer games to the vivid, hyper-reasonable virtual conditions of today. The account unfurls as an enrapturing investigation of how clownfish have changed from simple virtual elements to necessary characters that impact ongoing interaction, narrating, and player commitment.

2. **Overcoming any barrier: Sea life Science and Gaming Innovation**
   A focal motivation behind the book is to overcome any barrier between sea life science and gaming innovation. By analyzing the cooperation between sea life scholars and game designers, perusers gain bits of knowledge into the careful endeavors to really address clownfish and their submerged environments. This collaboration between logical exactness and innovative articulation upgrades the gaming experience as well as cultivates a more profound comprehension of marine life among players.

3. **Sustaining Ecological Mindfulness through Gaming**
   Past the pixels and interactivity mechanics, the book tries to feature the capability of gaming as an integral asset for supporting ecological mindfulness. The virtual seas where clownfish skip around become vivid homerooms, imparting in players a feeling of obligation for true marine protection. The intention is to grandstand how gaming, when utilized insightfully, can rise above diversion, turning into an impetus for positive ecological activity and stewardship.

4. **Examining the Social Effect of Clownfish in Gaming**
   A basic part of the book's motivation is the examination concerning the social effect of clownfish in gaming. The notable portrayal of these marine animals, filled by famous movies like "Tracking down Nemo," has penetrated worldwide culture.
   The story investigates how virtual portrayals of clownfish add to forming public impression of marine life, affecting gamers as well as society at large. The book tries to investigate the gradually expanding influences of these advanced portrayals on the social scene.

5. **Teaching Through Amusement: The Instructive Worth of Virtual Marine Conditions**
   In its quest for reason, the book stresses the instructive worth implanted inside virtual marine conditions. Gaming, frequently viewed as a type of diversion, arises as a powerful instructive medium. Perusers dig into the manners by which gaming encounters highlighting clownfish act as instructive devices, cultivating interest and figuring out about sea life science, environments, and preservation. The book highlights the harmonious connection among diversion and instruction, situating gaming as an entryway to information.

6. **Difficulties and Debates: Exploring the Moral Waters**
   Tending to difficulties and debates inside the convergence of gaming and marine life is a vital reason for the book. Moral worries, creative freedoms, and the possible effect of gaming on certifiable biological systems request insightful investigation. By exploring these moral waters, the book expects to work with a nuanced conversation,

empowering perusers to fundamentally survey the obligations of the gaming business in depicting marine life while keeping up with the creative liberty that characterizes the medium.

7. Future Prospects: Rousing Development and Cooperation

The book unfurls as a forward-looking investigation, imagining the future prospects and developments in the domain of gaming and marine portrayal. The object isn't just to hypothesize on the direction of virtual seas yet additionally to move development and cooperation between assorted partners. By imagining a future where gaming keeps on developing as a power for positive change, the book tries to propel perusers to effectively take part in the crossing point of science, gaming, and protection.

Chapter 1

The Origins Of Gaming And Virtual Realms

The tale of gaming and virtual domains is a captivating excursion that traverses many years, winding through mechanical progressions, social movements, and human inventiveness. To comprehend the virtual scenes we investigate today, it's significant to dig into the underlying foundations of gaming. This account starts during the twentieth hundred years, following the development of gaming from straightforward, simple entertainments to the vivid virtual domains we explore today.

The Beginning of Gaming

The early seeds of gaming were established in the post-The Second Great War time, as researchers and specialists began exploring different avenues regarding electronic gadgets. One of the earliest models was the cathode-beam tube entertainment gadget, made by physicist Thomas T. Goldsmith Jr. also, engineer Estle Beam Mann in 1947. This gadget, however essential by current norms, laid the foundation for intuitive electronic amusement.

The Introduction of Computer games

The genuine birth of computer games can be credited to the making of the principal monetarily effective arcade game, "Pong," created by Atari in 1972. Planned by Nolan Bushnell and delivered as an arcade game, "Pong" denoted a defining moment by bringing electronic gaming into public spaces. The straightforwardness of skipping a virtual ball to and fro resounded with crowds and prepared for the computer game industry.

Home Control center and the Gaming Insurgency

As innovation kept on propelling, the gaming experience changed from arcades to family rooms with the presentation of home gaming consoles. Magnavox Odyssey, delivered in 1972, is viewed as the principal home computer game control center. This undeniable the start of another time, permitting players to appreciate intelligent amusement inside the solace of their homes.

The Ascent of PCs

At the same time, the ascent of PCs in the last part of the 1970s and mid 1980s extended the opportunities for gaming. Games like "Space Trespassers" and "Pac-Man" became social peculiarities, catching the minds of millions. The approach of designs and sound cards in PCs further upgraded the gaming experience, pushing limits and making way for additional many-sided virtual domains.

Text-Based Undertakings and Pretending Games

In the beginning of individualized computing, text-based undertakings and pretending games (RPGs) assumed a critical part in molding virtual domains. Games like "Goliath Cavern Experience" and "Zork" connected with players through account driven encounters, laying the basis for the vivid narrating pervasive in contemporary gaming.

The Control center Conflicts and 3D Illustrations

The last part of the 1980s and mid 1990s saw the rise of the "console battles" between industry monsters Nintendo and Sega. This opposition energized advancement, prompting the improvement of 16-digit consoles like the Super Nintendo Theater setup (SNES) and the Sega Beginning. Moreover, progressions in 3D illustrations, exemplified by games like "Super Mario 64" and "Burial place Bandit," carried another aspect to virtual domains.

The Web and Multiplayer Gaming

The late twentieth century saw the broad reception of the web, opening new outskirts for gaming. Multiplayer web based games turned into a reality, with titles like "Shake" and "Ultima Internet" permitting players to associate and contend in virtual spaces. This noticeable an extraordinary second, as gaming developed from a lone encounter to a social action with worldwide ramifications.

The Period of Portable Gaming

The 21st century introduced the period of portable gaming, with the ascent of cell phones and tablets. Games like "Irate Birds" and "Flappy Bird" showed the availability and mass allure of versatile gaming, contacting crowds a long ways past conventional gaming socioeconomics. The omnipresence of cell phones changed virtual domains into versatile, in a hurry encounters.

The Introduction of Computer generated Reality

While computer generated reality (VR) had been an idea for many years, late years have seen huge headways in VR innovation. Gadgets like the Oculus Break and PlayStation VR have carried vivid encounters to the very front, permitting players to step into virtual domains more than ever.

VR has re-imagined the limits of gaming, offering a degree of inundation that was once the stuff of sci-fi.

The Effect of Increased Reality

Lined up with VR, increased reality (AR) has arisen as a momentous innovation. Games like "Pokémon GO" showed the capability of mixing virtual components with this present reality. AR has the ability to change our ordinary environmental factors into dynamic gaming conditions, obscuring the lines between the physical and virtual domains.

The Advancement of Gaming Stories

As innovation progressed, so did the intricacy of gaming stories. Narrating in computer games advanced from straightforward plots to perplexing, genuinely thunderous encounters. Games like "The Legend of Zelda: Breath of Nature" and "The Remainder of Us" showed the story capability of the medium, lifting gaming to a fine art equipped for conveying strong, vivid stories.

The Social Impact of Gaming

Gaming has risen above its status as a specialty side interest, turning into a social peculiarity with a worldwide effect. Esports rivalries fill arenas, and gaming shows draw in huge number of devotees. The impact of gaming stretches out past amusement, forming design, music, and even language, as gaming-related terms become coordinated into ordinary discussions.

The Job of Non mainstream Games

The ascent of non mainstream games in the late twentieth and mid 21st hundreds of years infused new imagination into the gaming scene. Free engineers, unrestricted by corporate requirements, delivered inventive and trial titles. Games like "Mesh," "Limbo," and "Undertale" showed the way that convincing encounters could emerge out of little, enthusiastic groups with exceptional dreams.

Gaming as a Social Peculiarity

The appearance of online multiplayer and social stages has changed gaming into a mutual movement. Players associate across borders, shaping networks and kinships inside virtual domains. Stages like Jerk and YouTube have transformed gaming into passive activities, with millions checking out watch their #1 players and characters.

Moral and Cultural Contemplations

As gaming's impact has developed, so affect society. Banters about brutality in computer games, compulsion concerns, and inclusivity inside the gaming local area have started significant discussions.

The business wrestles with the obligation that accompanies its social impact, prompting continuous discoursed about portrayal, variety, and moral game plan.

Virtual Domains and Idealism

Virtual domains give a space to idealism, permitting people to submerge themselves in substitute real factors. The allure of investigating fantastical universes, expecting various characters, and beating difficulties resounds with a different crowd. Gaming turns into a type of intuitive workmanship, offering a break from the unremarkable while giving open doors to self-revelation and self-improvement.

The Eventual fate of Gaming and Virtual Domains

Looking forward, the fate of gaming holds vast conceivable outcomes. Headways in man-made brainpower, computer generated reality, and expanded reality vow to push the limits of what is feasible. As gaming keeps on advancing, it will probably assume a necessary part in forming how we experience amusement, collaborate with innovation, and see the line between the genuine and the virtual.

1.1 Early Video Game History

The beginning of computer games denoted a groundbreaking second in the realm of diversion and innovation. From humble starting points as trial gadgets to the extravagant business it is today, the historical backdrop of early computer games is a captivating excursion through development, inventiveness, and the determined quest for intelligent encounters. This thorough investigation follows the underlying foundations of computer games, from the absolute first electronic diversions to the development of notable titles that established the groundwork for the gaming scene we know today.

The Introduction of Electronic Entertainments

The idea of electronic entertainments originates before the proper advancement of computer games. In the mid twentieth hundred years, creators and architects started exploring different avenues regarding electromechanical gadgets intended to engage and entertain. Outstanding models incorporate pinball machines and electro-mechanical arcade games like "Mutoscope," which depended on moving pictures and basic communications.

The Cathode-Beam Cylinder Entertainment Gadget

The genuine forerunner to video games arose in 1947 with the production of the cathode-beam tube entertainment gadget by physicist Thomas T. Goldsmith Jr. furthermore, engineer Estle Beam Mann. This early creation highlighted a simple gadget that permitted players to control a spot of light on the screen, pointing it at targets.

While essential by present day norms, this cathode-beam tube gadget laid the calculated basis for future electronic gaming.

The NIMROD PC and the Beginning of Computerized Gaming

During the 1950s, as PCs turned out to be more common, the potential for advanced gaming started to appear. The NIMROD PC, created in 1951 by Ferranti Worldwide for the Celebration of England, highlighted a game called NIM. This was one of the earliest cases of computerized gaming, as players could participate in a numerical procedure game on a modernized stage.

Spacewar! furthermore, the Introduction of PC Gaming Society

The mid 1960s saw the introduction of "Spacewar!" at the Massachusetts Establishment of Innovation (MIT). Created by Steve Russell, Martin Graetz, and Wayne Wiitanen, this pivotal game permitted two players to control spaceships and participate in a dueling fight in the profundities of room. "Spacewar!" exhibited the capability of PC gaming as well as laid out the establishment for a beginning gaming society, with lovers sharing the game on early PC organizations.

The Odyssey Control center: Birth of Home Video Gaming

The genuine upset in computer game history started with the arrival of the Magnavox Odyssey, the principal home computer game control center, in 1972. Created by Ralph Baer, the Odyssey permitted players to appreciate straightforward games like Pong and Hockey on their TVs. This noticeable a huge shift from the time of only arcade-based gaming to the presentation of intelligent diversion in the lounge.

The Ascent of Arcade Games

All the while, the 1970s saw the ascent of arcade games, which became social peculiarities. Nolan Bushnell and Ted Dabney established Atari in 1972 and delivered the notorious game "Pong" in 1972. This basic yet habit-forming table tennis reproduction enamored crowds and became one of the principal industrially fruitful arcade games. "Pong" laid the basis for the arcade blast of the last part of the '70s and mid '80s.

The Brilliant Period of Arcade Games

The last part of the 1970s and mid 1980s are frequently alluded to as the Brilliant Period of Arcade Games. During this period, arcades became social centers, drawing in players, everything being equal. Games like "Space Intruders," "Pac-Man," and "Jackass Kong" became notable, with characters like Pac-Man rising above the gaming scene to turn out to be mainstream society images. The progress of these games energized the development of the computer game industry.

The Home Computer game Accident of 1983

Notwithstanding the outcome of arcade games, the home control center market confronted a huge mishap in 1983 with the scandalous computer game accident. An immersion of bad quality games, oversaturation of the market, and rivalry from PCs prompted a decrease in buyer certainty.

Central parts like Atari confronted monetary difficulties, and the business saw a sharp constriction.

The Nintendo Theater setup (NES) Resurgence

The computer game industry tracked down its hero as the Nintendo Theater setup (NES). Delivered in 1985, the NES renewed the home control center market with hit titles like "Super Mario Brothers." and "The Legend of Zelda." Nintendo's tough quality control and permitting approaches reestablished customer trust and set up for the business' resurgence.

The Development of PCs

While the control center market recuperated, PCs likewise assumed a urgent part in molding the scene of early computer games. Organizations like IBM and Apple added to the development of PC gaming. Experience games, for example, "Enormous Cavern Experience" and "Zork," became well known, establishing the groundwork for story driven gaming encounters.

The Sonic versus Mario Period

The mid 1990s saw the opposition between Sega's Sonic the Hedgehog and Nintendo's Mario as the essence of control center gaming. This period became known for the "console battles," with Sega Beginning and Super Nintendo Theater setup (SNES) engaging for predominance. The competition among Sonic and Mario energized development and drove progressions in illustrations, sound, and ongoing interaction.

The Development of Designs and Sound

Headways in designs and sound were crucial in the development of computer games. The progress from 2D to 3D illustrations during the 1990s, exemplified by games like "Super Mario 64" and "Burial place Thief," denoted a progressive shift. The vivid universes made conceivable by further developed designs and sound innovation upgraded the gaming experience, enamoring players in phenomenal ways.

The Ascent of Compact disc ROMs and Realistic Encounters

The last part of the 1980s and mid 1990s saw the ascent of Compact disc ROM innovation, giving more than adequate capacity to bigger game documents and empowering the incorporation of full-movement video and voice acting.

Games like "Last Dream VII" and "Metal Stuff Strong" showed the potential for realistic narrating inside the gaming medium, setting new guidelines for account profundity.

The Approach of Online Multiplayer Gaming

The last part of the 1990s saw the appearance of online multiplayer gaming, as expanding web network permitted players to around the world interface. Games like "Tremor" and "StarCraft" became pioneers in the web based gaming space, cultivating a feeling of local area and contest among players. This obvious a huge shift from lone gaming encounters to social cooperations inside virtual domains.

The New Thousand years: Control center, Versatile Gaming, and Independent Transformation

The 21st century carried a huge number of changes to the gaming scene. The send off of the PlayStation 2, Xbox, and Nintendo GameCube flagged another time of control center gaming. At the same time, the ascent of portable gaming, impelled by cell phones and tablets, acquainted gaming with a more extensive crowd. Autonomous designers, or non mainstream game makers, acquired conspicuousness, carrying new and imaginative titles to the market.

Movement Controls and Computer generated Reality

Developments in gaming connection points have persistently formed the player experience. The presentation of movement controls with the Nintendo Wii in 2006 and the advancement of computer generated reality (VR) with gadgets like Oculus Break and PlayStation VR have additionally extended the opportunities for vivid interactivity. These innovations address a union of gaming and true actual connection.

The Social Effect of Esports

The 21st century has seen the ascent of esports, transforming cutthroat gaming into a worldwide peculiarity. Esports competitions fill arenas, with a great many watchers tuning in on the web. Games like "Class of Legends," "Dota 2," and "Fortnite" have become social standards, and expert gamers have accomplished VIP status. The incorporation of esports into standard culture mirrors the advancing meaning of gaming.

Moral and Cultural Contemplations

As computer games turned into a basic piece of standard culture, moral and cultural contemplations arose. Banters about savagery in computer games, worries about habit, and conversations in regards to portrayal and inclusivity inside the gaming business have become conspicuous. The business wrestles with its effect on society, provoking continuous discussions about mindful game plan and the effect of gaming on people.

1.2 Emergence of Virtual Environments

The rise of virtual conditions denotes a critical second in the direction of innovation, changing the manner in which people draw in with data, diversion, and each other. This investigation will dig into the complex advancement of virtual conditions, following their beginnings from simple programmatic experiences to the vivid and interconnected virtual universes we explore today.

1. Early Virtual experiences
   The Foundations of Virtual Conditions
   The incipient phases of virtual conditions can be followed back to the early analyses with PC created recreations. During the twentieth hundred years, pioneers started investigating the potential outcomes of establishing counterfeit conditions inside the computerized domain. These trailblazers laid the foundation for what might later become vivid virtual encounters.

   Early endeavors zeroed in on mimicking certifiable situations, introducing another time of PC helped preparing and recreation. Ventures, for example, flying and medical services embraced these advances for preparing, permitting experts to participate in practical situations without certifiable results.

   Military and Logical Applications
   The military immediately perceived the capability of virtual conditions for preparing and vital recreations. Early virtual experiences became significant instruments for planning troopers and officers for different situations. The marriage of innovation and military preparation upgraded readiness as well as pushed the limits of what PCs could accomplish.

   At the same time, virtual conditions tracked down applications in logical areas. Specialists and researchers utilized these reproductions for tests and investigations that were generally unrealistic or unimaginable in the actual world. The rise of virtual conditions as a device for logical request proclaimed another period in research strategies.

2. Augmented Reality (VR) and Head-Mounted Showcases
   The Introduction of Computer generated Reality
   The genuine defining moment in the advancement of virtual conditions accompanied the beginning of augmented reality (VR). Ivan Sutherland's visionary idea, the "Sword of Damocles," presented head-mounted shows, a fundamental component in the vivid VR experience. This idea established the groundwork for a change in outlook in how people collaborated with computerized spaces.

   In spite of the earth shattering idea, early VR confronted critical difficulties and impediments. Innovative requirements, for example, restricted handling power and unrefined designs, blocked the consistent making of vivid virtual conditions. Notwithstanding, the visionaries of the time, motivated by sci-fi accounts, kept on pushing the limits of what was innovatively achievable.

   Commercialization and Diversion
   The progress from hypothetical ideas to useful utilizations of

augmented reality happened during the arcade period. Early endeavors to bring VR encounters to the majority appeared as arcade arrangements, permitting people to step into virtual universes for brief and exciting experiences. These encounters, while historic, were obliged by the innovative restrictions of the time.

The development of virtual conditions in media outlets resembled progressions in figuring power. As innovation improved, so did the potential for making more modern and vivid computer generated simulation encounters. Head-mounted shows turned out to be more refined, and VR began to reach out past arcades into homes, offering buyers a sample of the computerized domains.

3. **Expanded Reality (AR) and Blended Reality (MR)**

Growing Real factors

While computer generated reality expected to establish completely manufactured conditions, the rise of increased reality (AR) acquainted another aspect with the advanced insight. AR overlays advanced data onto this present reality, mixing the physical and virtual consistently. This innovation tracked down applications across different enterprises, from gaming to training and medical services.

The idea of blended reality (MR) further obscured the lines between the physical and advanced domains. MR coordinates virtual and expanded reality components into the client's genuine climate, making an intelligent and dynamic space where computerized and actual items coincide and associate.

Business and Modern Applications

AR and MR tracked down useful applications in business and modern settings. In fields, for example, assembling and upkeep, AR advancements became instrumental in giving constant data and direction to laborers. The capacity to overlay computerized directions onto actual articles smoothed out processes and worked on by and large productivity.

The gaming business additionally embraced AR, with games like "Pokemon GO" exhibiting the potential for mixing computerized encounters with this present reality. This mix of virtual components into day to day existence denoted a critical change in how people cooperated with and saw their environmental factors.

4. **The Ascent of Virtual Conditions in Gaming**

From Pixels to Drenching

Virtual conditions tracked down a characteristic home in the domain of gaming. The development of computer games from pixelated illustrations to vivid 3D universes resembled progressions in virtual climate advances. The presentation of strong designs cards, high-goal shows, and refined gaming motors prepared for phenomenal degrees of submersion.

Early gaming encounters only alluded to the capability of virtual conditions. As innovation advanced, game designers embraced the test of making sweeping and practical computerized universes. Games like "Universe of Warcraft" and "The Senior Parchments: Skyrim" shipped players to complicatedly definite domains, offering a sample of the vivid encounters virtual conditions could give.

Computer generated Reality in Gaming

The reconciliation of computer generated reality into gaming addressed a seismic change in how players drew in with computerized universes. VR headsets, outfitted with movement following and haptic input, permitted clients to step inside their number one games. This degree of drenching made unrivaled encounters, whether investigating outsider scenes or doing combating enemies in a dream domain.

The gaming business' hug of VR went past conventional kinds. Augmented reality took into consideration the formation of extraordinary and trial titles that pushed the limits of narrating, connection, and profound commitment. Games like "Beat Saber" and "Half-Life: Alyx" exhibited the flexibility and capability of virtual conditions in gaming.

5. ## Social Virtual Conditions

Interfacing Past Limits

Virtual conditions advanced from singular encounters to social stages, empowering clients to associate and cooperate with others in computerized spaces. Social virtual conditions rose above geological limits, permitting people from around the world to share encounters, team up, and structure networks.

Online multiplayer games assumed a huge part in cultivating social communications inside virtual domains. Games like "Fortnite" and "Minecraft" became gaming stages as well as friendly center points where players could team up, contend, and make together. The development of virtual social spaces denoted a significant change in how individuals shaped connections and drew in with computerized content.

Virtual Gatherings and Conferencing

The worldwide shift towards remote work and virtual correspondence further sped up the reception of social virtual conditions. Virtual gatherings and meetings, worked with by stages like Zoom and Microsoft Groups, became basic pieces of expert and instructive settings. Symbols and virtual spaces gave a feeling of presence and commitment that conventional video conferencing needed.

6. Challenges and Moral Contemplations

Specialized Obstacles and Openness

While the advancement of virtual conditions has been exceptional, it has not been without challenges. Specialized obstacles, for example, dormancy issues in augmented simulation and the requirement for strong equipment, have restricted far and wide reception. Openness stays a worry, with the expense of very good quality VR gear going about as a hindrance for a few possible clients.

Moral Contemplations

As virtual conditions become more imbued in our day to day routines, moral contemplations come to the front. Issues connected with protection, security, and the potential for dependence bring up issues about the mindful turn of events and utilization of virtual advancements. Finding some kind of harmony among development and moral contemplations is essential as these innovations keep on progressing.

7. Future Patterns and Advancements

Innovative Progressions

Looking forward, the eventual fate of virtual conditions guarantees proceeded with advancement and refinement. Headways in registering power, illustrations capacities, and man-made reasoning will probably add to additional practical and dynamic virtual universes. The continuous improvement of haptic input frameworks and more vivid points of interaction could additionally upgrade the tactile experience inside virtual conditions.

Combination of Man-made brainpower

The combination of man-made brainpower (simulated intelligence) into virtual conditions holds huge potential. Computer based intelligence driven characters and dynamic, responsive conditions could make more similar and drawing in encounters. This combination of virtual conditions and simulated intelligence can possibly reform gaming as well as schooling, medical care, and different businesses.

Extended Applications in Medical care and Training

Virtual conditions have previously shown their worth in medical services and training, and future developments are probably going to extend these applications. Careful recreations, virtual clinical conferences, and vivid instructive encounters could turn out to be more complex and broadly embraced. Computer generated reality and expanded reality can possibly change preparing and schooling across different fields.

Blockchain and Virtual Economies

The joining of blockchain innovation into virtual conditions might introduce additional opportunities for virtual economies. Blockchain can give secure and straightforward exchanges inside virtual spaces, empowering the creation and exchange of advanced resources. This could have suggestions for gaming, virtual land, and other virtual commercial centers.

1.3Influence of Nature in Gaming

The impact of nature in gaming is a diverse and charming viewpoint that has developed close by the computer game industry's development. From the beginning of pixelated scenes to the vivid open universes of today, nature has been a steady wellspring of motivation for game designers. This investigation dives into the different ways nature appears in gaming, forming scenes, stories, characters, and, surprisingly, game mechanics.

1. **Regular Scenes in Gaming**

   The Advancement of Illustrations and Portrayal

   In the beginning of gaming, graphical limits restricted the portrayal of nature to straightforward pixelated conditions. Games like "Experience" on the Atari 2600 portrayed conceptual scenes that indicated regular components. As innovation progressed, the depiction of nature went through an extraordinary shift.

   Progressions in designs innovation considered more reasonable and definite portrayals of regular scenes. Games like "The Legend of Zelda: Ocarina of Time" and "Last Dream VII" displayed rich timberlands, extensive fields, and glorious mountains. These outwardly staggering conditions filled in as backgrounds as well as became vital parts of the gaming experience.

   Open-World Investigation

   The development of open-world games denoted a critical achievement in the portrayal of nature in gaming. Titles like "The Senior Parchments: Skyrim" and "The Legend of Zelda: Breath of Nature" introduced immense, consistent scenes that players could investigate openly. The vivid idea of these virtual universes made a feeling of stunningness and miracle, catching the quintessence of certifiable normal excellence.

   Natural Variety

   Nature in gaming isn't restricted to conventional scenes however stretches out to assorted biological systems and biomes. Games like "Red Dead Recovery 2" carefully reproduce different regular living spaces, from thick woodlands and dry deserts to frigid mountains and submerged domains. The consideration regarding ecological va riety upgrades the feeling of authenticity and furnishes players with fluctuated and outwardly charming encounters.

2. Greenery in Gaming

Flower Style

The portrayal of greenery in gaming goes past simple foundation components. Games frequently highlight unpredictable and out-wardly engaging vegetation, from fantastical blossoms in mystical domains to sensible foliage in endurance games. The stylish charac-teristics of in-game greenery add to the in general visual allure and climate of virtual conditions.

Fauna and Untamed life Association

Untamed life in gaming adds an additional layer of dynamism to virtual scenes. Games like "Long ways" and "Red Dead Reclamation 2" mimic biological systems with different fauna, permitting players to experience and associate with natural life. The way of behaving of virtual creatures, their job in the game's biological system, and the difficulties they present add to a more vivid and connecting with experience.

Natural Elements

A few games go past static portrayals of verdure, consolidating biological elements. "Spore," for instance, permits players to direct the development of animals, affecting their attributes and ways of behaving. This environmental angle adds profundity to the gaming experience and underscores the interconnectedness of nature.

3. Nature as a Story Component

Laying everything out

Nature assumes a pivotal part in forming the story of many games. Whether it's the thick wildernesses of "Strange: Drake's Fortune" or the dystopian wild of "The Remainder of Us," normal settings add to the general environment and narrating. The visual and hear-able components of nature become narrating apparatuses, establishing the vibe and upgrading the close to home effect of the story.

Imagery and Illustration

Nature is much of the time utilized emblematically in gaming stories. Emblematic portrayals of seasons, climate, and normal peculiarities can convey more profound implications. For instance, the changing seasons in "Excursion" mirror the repetitive idea of life, while the climate in "Weighty Downpour" fills in as an illustration for the personal unrest of the characters.

Ecological Narrating

Past filling in as a scenery, nature can effectively take part in ecological narrating. Deserted structures in congested scenes, endured ruins recovered essentially, and indications of biological movements recount quiet accounts of civilizations and occasions that molded the game world. This strategy adds layers of story profundity that players can uncover through investigation.

4. Normal Components in Game Mechanics

Dynamic Climate Frameworks

Advancements in game mechanics have permitted engineers to coordinate unique climate frameworks. Games like "The Legend of Zelda: Breath of Nature" highlight sensible atmospheric conditions that influence ongoing interaction. Downpour can make surfaces tricky, influencing route, while tempests can impact battle and the way of behaving of in-game animals. Dynamic weather conditions adds a component of capriciousness, causing the virtual world to feel more invigorated.

Day-Night Cycles

The joining of day-night cycles in gaming improves authenticity and drenching. Normal lighting changes over the course of the day, influencing perceivability and the general air. Games like "Minecraft" and "The Witcher 3: Wild Chase" use day-night cycles for tasteful purposes as well as a utilitarian perspective that impacts interactivity, like the way of behaving of specific animals or the accessibility of specific missions.

Endurance Mechanics

Nature's impact stretches out to endurance games, where players should battle with the components to make due. Games like "Don't Starve" and "The Long Dim" present mechanics like temperature, appetite, and endurance, driving players to decisively collaborate with the virtual climate. The consideration of endurance components adds a layer of authenticity and challenge to ongoing interaction.

5. Nature as a Wellspring of Motivation

Creative Motivation

Game engineers frequently draw motivation from the magnificence of the normal world for imaginative plan. From amazing dusks and brilliant evenings to the energetic shades of coral reefs, nature's range is reflected in the visuals of many games. Creative translations of nature add to the general feel and allure of virtual conditions.

Design Motivation

Past scenes, nature impacts building plan in virtual universes. Games like "The Legend of Zelda: Breath of Nature" highlight structures flawlessly coordinated with the common habitat. Treehouses, caves, and cliffside homes mix compositional imagination with the natural structures tracked down in nature.

6. Natural Mindfulness and Protection in Gaming

Advancing Natural Cognizance

A few games influence virtual conditions to bring issues to light about true ecological issues. "Destiny of the World" and "Eco" challenge players to settle on choices that influence the virtual biological system, featuring the outcomes of human activities on the climate. These games act as instructive apparatuses, advancing ecological cognizance and starting conversations about supportability.

Cooperation with Protection Associations

The gaming business has likewise teamed up with preservation associations to advance certifiable ecological drives. Games like "Universe of Warcraft" have presented virtual pets or mounts as a feature of noble cause crusades, with continues supporting preservation endeavors. This crossing point between virtual universes and certifiable protection exhibits the potential for gaming to contribute emphatically to ecological causes.

7. Difficulties and Potential open doors

Adjusting Authenticity and Dream

While the impact of nature in gaming has prompted outwardly dazzling and vivid encounters, there's a consistent test in adjusting authenticity with the fantastical. Finding some kind of harmony guarantees that games give spellbinding virtual conditions while considering inventive articulation and innovative narrating.

Innovative Requirements and Headways

Mechanical imperatives, for example, restricted handling power and capacity limit, have generally impacted the portrayal of nature in gaming. Nonetheless, progressing headways in illustrations innovation, augmented reality, and man-made reasoning present energizing open doors for considerably more practical and intelligent virtual conditions.

Moral Contemplations

As games become more modern in their portrayal of nature, moral contemplations come to the very front. The dependable utilization of virtual conditions includes addressing concerns connected with ecological effect, social awareness, and the potential for supporting unsafe generalizations or stories.

8. Future Patterns and Potential outcomes

Headways in Computer generated Experience and Expanded Reality

What's in store holds energizing opportunities for virtual conditions, especially with headways in computer generated experience (VR) and expanded reality (AR). VR innovation keeps on improving, offering more vivid encounters that bring players considerably nearer to nature. AR, then again, can possibly mix virtual and genuine components flawlessly, improving ordinary encounters.

Joining of Computerized reasoning

The joining of computerized reasoning (man-made intelligence) into gaming conditions is probably going to shape more powerful and responsive virtual biological systems. Computer based intelligence driven characters, weather conditions, and natural frameworks could make more sensible and developing virtual universes, where the activities of players lastingly affect the climate.

Extension of Instructive and Helpful Applications

Virtual conditions have huge undiscovered possibility in instructive and restorative applications. From vivid nature-based growth opportunities for understudies to virtual conditions intended for unwinding and stress help, the opportunities for positive effect on psychological well-being and prosperity are broad.

Chapter 2

Clownfish In The Real World

The clownfish, with its dynamic tones and one of a kind ways of behaving, stands apart as quite possibly of the most famous marine animal. Generally perceived for its relationship with coral reefs and promoted by energized motion pictures, this present reality clownfish is an intriguing animal varieties that possesses the world's seas. This investigation plans to give an exhaustive comprehension of clownfish right at home, diving into their science, conduct, natural jobs, and the preservation challenges they face.

1. Scientific categorization and Characterization
   Logical Characterization
   Clownfish have a place with the family Pomacentridae inside the request Perciformes. The family Pomacentridae is usually known as damselfishes, and clownfish are a subgroup inside this family. The most notable types of clownfish have a place with the Amphiprioninae subfamily, with the sort Amphiprion containing different species.
   Species Variety
   The variety Amphiprion incorporates north of 30 perceived types of clownfish, each with its special attributes and dispersion. The absolute most remarkable species incorporate the Ocellaris clownfish (Amphiprion ocellaris), Percula clownfish (Amphiprion percula), and the Tomato clownfish (Amphiprion frenatus). The particular markings and hue of every species add to their allure in both logical review and mainstream society.
2. Dispersion and Natural surroundings
   Worldwide Reach
   Clownfish are principally tracked down in the warm waters of the

Pacific and Indian Seas. Their dispersion stretches out from the Incomparable Obstruction Reef in Australia to the Red Ocean and the western Pacific islands. Outstandingly, they are missing from the Atlantic Sea, restricting their worldwide reach to explicit districts portrayed by coral reefs.

Coral Reef Conditions

Clownfish are firmly connected with coral reefs, especially the shallow, safeguarded tidal ponds and coral-rich environments. They structure harmonious associations with different types of ocean anemones, looking for shelter inside the arms of these living beings. The concurrence of clownfish and ocean anemones is a momentous illustration of mutualism, where the two species benefit from the affiliation.

3. ## Science and Life structures

    ## Morphology

    Clownfish display particular morphological highlights that add to their exceptional appearance. They are portrayed by their little size, commonly going from 2 to 5 crawls long. The body is horizontally packed, and the dorsal balance reaches out into a progression of spines. The most striking component is their energetic shading, frequently comprising of intense orange, white, and dark examples. These varieties fill different needs, including correspondence, cover, and species acknowledgment.

    ## Advantageous Connection with Ocean Anemones

    One of the most striking parts of clownfish science is their advantageous connection with ocean anemones. While the limbs of ocean anemones contain particular stinging cells called nematocysts, clownfish are safeguarded from these stings because of a layer of bodily fluid on their skin. As a trade-off for sanctuary and insurance, clownfish offer food to the ocean anemones and assist with hindering polyp-eating hunters.

    ## Conceptive Procedures

    Clownfish are known for their fascinating regenerative systems. They are protandrous bisexuals, meaning they have both male and female regenerative organs. In a gathering of clownfish, the biggest and most prevailing individual is the female, the following biggest is the reproducing male, and the others are non-rearing guys. Without any the female, the rearing male can go through a sex change to turn into the new female.

4. ## Conduct and Social Design

    ## Order in Gatherings

    Clownfish display a mind boggling social design inside their gatherings. A prevailing reproducing pair, comprising of the biggest female and the biggest male, possesses the anemone. The pecking order is kept up with through forceful ways of behaving, with the predominant female being the highest level person. The reproducing male helps with safeguarding the region and really focuses on the eggs.

Correspondence and Vocalization

Correspondence among clownfish includes a mix of visual presentations, body developments, and vocalizations. They use popping and tweeting sounds delivered by grating their teeth to lay out region limits and impart inside the gathering. These acoustic signs assume a critical part in keeping up with the social design and staying away from clashes.

Defensive Ways of behaving

Clownfish are known for their defensive ways of behaving, particularly with regards to monitoring their eggs. The reproducing male constantly keeps an eye on the grasp of eggs, fanning them with his pectoral blades to guarantee appropriate oxygenation. Both the male and female enthusiastically guard the home from expected dangers, exhibiting momentous nurturing impulses.

5. Natural Jobs

Taking care of Propensities

Clownfish have omnivorous taking care of propensities, consuming an eating routine that incorporates little shellfish, zooplankton, and green growth. They assume a part in controlling populaces of these living beings inside their natural surroundings. Also, their cooperations with ocean anemones add to the general strength of coral reef biological systems.

Coral Reef Wellbeing

Clownfish are viewed as pointer species for the strength of coral reefs. Their reliance on coral reefs and aversion to natural changes make them important signs of environment prosperity. Factors like coral blanching, natural surroundings obliteration, and water quality straightforwardly influence clownfish populaces, giving specialists bits of knowledge into more extensive coral reef wellbeing.

6. Dangers and Protection Difficulties

Coral Fading and Environment Misfortune

One of the main dangers to clownfish and their biological systems is coral dying. Climbing ocean temperatures, credited to environmental change, can prompt the removal of advantageous green growth from coral tissues, causing blanching. As coral reefs corrupt, the accessibility of reasonable territories for clownfish decreases, influencing their populaces.

Assortment for the Aquarium Exchange

The fame of clownfish in the aquarium exchange represents a danger to wild populaces. Impractical assortment rehearses, where fish are caught for business purposes, can exhaust nearby populaces and disturb the fragile equilibrium of coral reef biological systems. Endeavors to manage and advance reasonable practices in the aquarium exchange are pivotal for the preservation of clownfish.

Sea Fermentation

Sea fermentation, a result of expanded carbon dioxide ingestion via seawater, represents a danger to marine life, including clownfish. Fermentation can adversely affect the advancement of clownfish hatchlings, influencing their capacity to settle and get by in coral reef conditions. Tending to the main drivers of sea fermentation is imperative for the drawn out protection of marine species.

7. Protection Endeavors

Marine Safeguarded Regions

The foundation of marine safeguarded regions (MPAs) assumes a basic part in clownfish protection. MPAs give places of refuge where environments can recuperate, and fish populaces, including clownfish, can flourish. All around oversaw MPAs add to the protection of biodiversity, support research endeavors, and act as models for feasible marine asset the board.

Feasible Fisheries The executives

Advancing supportable fisheries the executives is fundamental for keeping up with clownfish populaces. Carrying out guidelines and practices that forestall overfishing and limit bycatch helps safeguard the fragile equilibrium of coral reef environments. Economical administration approaches think about the necessities of both neighborhood networks and the marine climate.

Local area Commitment and Training

Local area commitment and training drives are instrumental in clownfish protection. Bringing issues to light about the natural significance of clownfish and their territories energizes dependable ways of behaving and encourages a feeling of stewardship among nearby networks. Training programs likewise assume an imperative part in advancing manageable the travel industry rehearses.

8. Future Possibilities and Exploration Bearings

Environment Strong Corals

Examination into creating environment tough corals holds guarantee for the future of clownfish and coral reef biological systems. Researchers are investigating hereditary and natural intercessions to improve the flexibility of corals to increasing ocean temperatures. These endeavors intend to make coral populaces that can more readily endure the effects of environmental change, helping related species like clownfish.

Progressions in Hydroponics

Headways in hydroponics procedures offer possible answers for diminishing the effect of the aquarium exchange on wild clownfish populaces. Practical reproducing programs in bondage can give a wellspring of clownfish to the aquarium exchange without depending on wild-gotten examples. Capable hydroponics rehearses add to preservation endeavors and diminish the tension on delicate marine biological systems.

2.1 Biology and Behavior of Clownfish

Clownfish, with their energetic varieties and unmistakable ways of behaving, have become notable figures in the realm of marine life. Made well known by energized motion pictures, these little, exotic fish are outwardly striking as well as captivating in their science and conduct. This investigation expects to give a top to bottom comprehension of the science and conduct of clownfish, diving into their life systems, conceptive methodologies, cooperative connections, correspondence, and environmental jobs.

1. Life structures and Morphology
   Actual Attributes
   Clownfish, having a place with the family Pomacentridae, are portrayed by their little size, commonly going from 2 to 5 crawls long. Their bodies are horizontally compacted, highlighting an unmistakable shading design that incorporates dazzling oranges, whites, and blacks. The one of a kind markings on their bodies fill both useful and stylish needs, helping with species acknowledgment and cover among coral reef conditions.
   The dorsal blade of clownfish reaches out into a progression of spines, and their pectoral balances are advanced, considering exact developments. The mouth is little and terminal, outfitted with sharp teeth utilized for benefiting from different little organic entities.
   Cooperative Relationship with Ocean Anemones
   One of the most entrancing parts of clownfish life systems is their harmonious relationship with ocean anemones. In spite of the stinging cells, or nematocysts, present on the arms of ocean anemones, clownfish are shielded from their sting. This insurance is credited to a layer of bodily fluid on the clownfish's skin that forestalls setting

off the nematocysts.

Clownfish coincide with a few types of ocean anemones, looking for shelter inside their limbs. This commonly valuable relationship includes the clownfish getting insurance from hunters, while the ocean anemones benefit from the food gave by the clownfish and assurance from polyp-eating hunters.

2. Regenerative Procedures

Protandrous Bisexuals

Clownfish are known for their one of a kind regenerative methodologies, especially their status as protandrous bisexuals. In a gathering of clownfish, the biggest and most prevailing individual is the female, the following biggest is the reproducing male, and the others are non-rearing guys. This social design is basic for the endurance and conceptive progress of the gathering.

Without the female, the rearing male can go through a sex change, progressing to turn into the new female. This variation guarantees the constant presence of a regenerative female inside the gathering. The progress includes physiological changes, like the advancement of female regenerative organs and modifications in conduct.

Romance and Match Holding

The romance and match holding customs of clownfish are multifaceted and include a progression of ways of behaving. The reproducing male draws in the female by performing visual presentations, including swimming movements and blade developments. Vocalizations, delivered by grating their teeth, likewise assume a part in romance correspondence.

When the pair has fortified, they take part in a dance-like way of behaving, orbiting around one another and the picked ocean anemone. This conduct fortifies the pair bond and lays an out their area inside the anemone. The female then, at that point, chooses a reasonable site for laying eggs, regularly on a level surface near the anemone.

Egg Care and Parental Way of behaving

Clownfish are determined guardians, and both the male and female are effectively associated with really focusing on the eggs. After the female lays the eggs, the male assumes on the liability of keeping an eye on them. Utilizing his pectoral blades, he fans the eggs to guarantee legitimate oxygenation and eliminates any flotsam and jetsam or likely dangers.

During the hatching time frame, which shifts among species, the male watches the eggs wildly. He protects the home from likely hunters and guarantees the prosperity of the creating undeveloped organisms. When the eggs hatch, the hatchlings float away with the flows until they are prepared to get comfortable a reasonable natural surroundings.

3. Social Design and Conduct inside Gatherings
Pecking order
Clownfish display a perplexing social design inside their gatherings, known as anemonefish states. The ordered progression inside these provinces depends on size, with the biggest female possessing the top position.

The rearing male, which is the second-biggest individual, helps the female in keeping up with strength and safeguarding the domain.

Non-rearing guys inside the gathering are more modest and subordinate. Their essential job is to assist with safeguarding the region and give help to the reproducing pair. Without even a trace of the female, the rearing male can go through a sex change, turning into the new female and guaranteeing the congruity of the conceptive cycle.

Agonistic Ways of behaving
Keeping up with the pecking order includes different agonistic ways of behaving, particularly between contending females. Forceful experiences, including gnawing, pursuing, and blade shows, are normal as people lay out and guard their position inside the gathering. These ways of behaving assist with controlling the social design and limit struggle inside the province.

Correspondence and Vocalization
Correspondence assumes a pivotal part in the social way of behaving of clownfish, and they utilize a blend of visual presentations, body developments, and vocalizations. Clownfish produce popping and tweeting sounds by grating their teeth together. These sounds serve numerous capabilities, including regional correspondence, romance ceremonies, and keeping up with attachment inside the gathering.

The particular acoustic signs shift among species, and people can perceive and answer the extraordinary hints of their gathering individuals. These vocalizations add to the foundation of domain limits and the coordination of gathering exercises.

4. Taking care of Propensities and Environmental Jobs
Omnivorous Eating regimen
Clownfish are omnivores, meaning they consume a different eating routine that incorporates both plant and creature matter. Their taking care of propensities are adjusted to their coral reef conditions, where they search for little scavangers, zooplankton, and green growth. The capacity to benefit from various life forms adds to their environmental job in controlling populaces of little spineless creatures inside coral reef biological systems.

Job in Coral Reef Wellbeing

Clownfish are viewed as vital participants in the strength of coral reefs. As they rummage for food, they assist with directing populaces of creatures like zooplankton and little scavangers. Furthermore, their harmonious relationship with ocean anemones adds to the general wellbeing and equilibrium of coral reef biological systems.

The stool of clownfish likewise fills in as a wellspring of supplements for the ocean anemones, improving the development and prosperity of these harmonious accomplices. By taking part in supplement cycling, clownfish have an impact in the perplexing snare of collaborations that characterize the biological elements of coral reef conditions.

5. **Dangers and Preservation Difficulties**

Coral Fading and Environment Misfortune

One of the essential dangers to clownfish populaces is coral fading, a peculiarity related with climbing ocean temperatures. Environmental change adds to expanded ocean temperatures, prompting the removal of advantageous green growth from coral tissues. Subsequently, the coral becomes white, loses its energy, and turns out to be more helpless to infection.

Coral dying influences the strength of coral reefs as well as reduces the accessibility of appropriate natural surroundings for clownfish. The deficiency of coral reefs due to dying and different elements, for example, environment obliteration and contamination, represents a critical preservation challenge.

Assortment for the Aquarium Exchange

The prominence of clownfish in the aquarium exchange has prompted worries about over-assortment from nature. Impractical collecting practices can drain neighborhood populaces and disturb the sensitive equilibrium of coral reef biological systems. The interest for clownfish in the aquarium exchange features the requirement for economical and dependable practices to guarantee the preservation of wild populaces.

Sea Fermentation

Sea fermentation, coming about because of the retention of over-abundance carbon dioxide via seawater, represents a danger to marine life, including clownfish. Fermentation can influence the advancement of clownfish hatchlings, influencing their capacity to settle and make due in coral reef conditions. Tending to the main drivers of sea fermentation is pivotal for the drawn out preservation of marine species.

6. Preservation Endeavors
   Marine Safeguarded Regions
   The foundation of Marine Safeguarded Regions (MPAs) has been a vital protection methodology for clownfish and coral reef environments. MPAs give assigned regions where marine life, including clownfish, can flourish without the tensions of overfishing and living space corruption. Very much oversaw MPAs add to the protection of biodiversity and act as important apparatuses for specialists concentrating on marine environments.
   Supportable Fisheries The executives
   Advancing reasonable fisheries the executives is fundamental for keeping up with clownfish populaces. Executing guidelines and practices that forestall overfishing and limit bycatch assist with safeguarding the sensitive equilibrium of coral reef biological systems. Economical administration approaches think about the necessities of both neighborhood networks and the marine climate.
   Local area Commitment and Schooling
   Drawing in nearby networks and bringing issues to light about the significance of clownfish and coral reef environments is fundamental for protection endeavors. Instructive projects can illuminate networks about feasible practices, mindful the travel industry, and the biological jobs of clownfish. By encouraging a feeling of stewardship and natural obligation, local area commitment adds to long haul preservation achievement.
7. Future Exploration Headings

Environment Tough Corals
Research zeroed in on creating environment tough corals holds guarantee for the future preservation of clownfish and other marine species. Researchers are investigating hereditary and natural mediations to improve the strength of corals to increasing ocean temperatures. These endeavors expect to make coral populaces that can more readily endure the effects of environmental change, helping related species like clownfish.
Headways in Hydroponics
Progressions in hydroponics methods offer possible answers for diminishing the effect of the aquarium exchange on wild clownfish populaces. Feasible reproducing programs in bondage can give a wellspring of clownfish to the aquarium exchange without depending on wild-gotten examples. Mindful hydroponics rehearses add to protection endeavors and lessen the strain on delicate marine biological systems.
2.2Coral Reefs as Natural Habitats

Coral reefs stand as probably the most different and dynamic biological systems in the world, giving a home to a stunning cluster of marine life. These submerged wonderlands, frequently alluded to as the "rainforests of the ocean," assume a vital part in supporting biodiversity, supporting fisheries, and adding to the general wellbeing of the world's seas. This investigation dives into the multi-layered parts of coral reefs as normal territories, analyzing their arrangement, biodiversity, biological capabilities, the dangers they face, and continuous preservation endeavors.

1. Arrangement and Construction of Coral Reefs
   Coral Polyps and Coral Provinces
   At the core of coral reefs are coral polyps, little and fragile creatures that have a place with the class Anthozoa. These polyps discharge calcium carbonate to frame defensive skeletons, making the hard designs that we perceive as coral. Individual coral polyps might be minuscule, yet they combine to shape huge states, with every polyp adding to the development of the coral design.
   Kinds of Coral Reefs
   Coral reefs come in different structures, each formed by various ecological circumstances. The three fundamental kinds of coral reefs are bordering reefs, hindrance reefs, and atolls.
   Bordering Reefs: These are the most widely recognized type and straightforwardly line shores. They develop offshore, shaping a shallow stage along the shore.
   Obstruction Reefs: Found farther from the shore, boundary reefs are isolated from the land by more profound, vast water. Australia's Incredible Boundary Reef is a remarkable model.
   Atolls: Atolls are round coral reef developments that encompass a focal tidal pond. They frequently structure around the edge of lowered, wiped out volcanic islands.
2. Biodiversity in Coral Reefs
   Coral Reef Species
   Coral reefs are prestigious for their unprecedented biodiversity, facilitating a huge range of marine species. The many-sided construction of the coral gives various specialties to living beings to possess. Fish, spineless creatures, and green growth flourish in this mind boggling environment.
   Fish Variety: Coral reefs are home to a stunning variety of fish species, from brilliant reef fish like angelfish and parrotfish to huge hunters like groupers and sharks. The intricacy of the reef structure gives concealing spots, favorable places, and taking care of chances.

Spineless creatures: Spineless creatures like wipes, ocean anemones, and delicate corals add to the energetic mosaic of life on coral reefs. The cooperative connection between coral polyps and zooxanthellae, a sort of green growth, is a key part of coral reef biological systems.

Green growth and Plants: Green growth assume a vital part in coral reef environments. They are not just an essential food hotspot for some living beings yet additionally add to the energy balance through photosynthesis. Seagrasses and mangroves, however not straightforwardly a piece of the coral construction, are vital to the general strength of the reef framework.

Zooxanthellae and Coral Advantageous interaction

The organization between coral polyps and zooxanthellae is a foundation of coral reef environments. Zooxanthellae live inside the tissues of coral polyps, furnishing them with fundamental supplements through photosynthesis. Consequently, the coral polyps offer security and a steady climate for the zooxanthellae. This co-operative relationship is answerable for the dynamic tones seen in sound coral reefs and is pivotal for their endurance.

3. Biological Elements of Coral Reefs

Coral Reefs as Nurseries

Coral reefs act as crucial nurseries for the overwhelming majority marine species. The perplexing design of the reef gives haven and assurance to the early life phases of different fish and spineless creatures. Adolescent fish track down asylum in the little hiding spots of the reef, getting away from predation in the untamed sea. As they develop, these species might move to different natural surroundings, adding to the more extensive marine biological system.

Fisheries and Monetary Significance

Coral reefs assume a focal part in supporting fisheries and the occupations of waterfront networks. Numerous financially significant fish species depend on coral reefs for reproducing and taking care of grounds. The monetary worth of coral reefs reaches out past fisheries, as these environments draw in the travel industry, turning out revenue and business valuable open doors for nearby networks.

Safeguarding Coastlines and Forestalling Disintegration

The construction of coral reefs safeguards shorelines from the effect of waves and tempests. The complicated trap of coral branches and the living beings that occupy them disseminate wave energy, diminishing the power that arrives at the shore. This regular hindrance is fundamental for forestalling disintegration and keeping up with the respectability of seaside biological systems.

4. Dangers to Coral Reefs

Coral Blanching

One of the main dangers to coral reefs is coral blanching, a peculiarity connected to climbing ocean temperatures. At the point when corals experience delayed times of raised temperatures, they remove the advantageous zooxanthellae living in their tissues. This removal makes the coral lose its lively varieties, an indication of stress, and can prompt coral passing on the off chance that the unpleasant circumstances persevere.

Sea Fermentation

The retention of overabundance carbon dioxide via seawater prompts sea fermentation, a cycle that can adversely influence the capacity of corals to fabricate their skeletons. Coral skeletons are made out of calcium carbonate, and under acidic circumstances, these designs can disintegrate. Sea fermentation represents a drawn out danger to the uprightness of coral reef biological systems.

Overfishing and Damaging Fishing Practices

Overfishing, driven by the interest for fish, represents an immediate danger to the biodiversity of coral reefs. Impractical fishing rehearses, for example, the utilization of explosive or cyanide to catch fish, can make broad harm coral states and disturb the sensitive equilibrium of the biological system. The expulsion of key species from the food web can have flowing consequences for the whole reef local area.

Contamination and Spillover

Contamination from land-based sources, including rural overflow and metropolitan wastewater, brings supplements and impurities into coral reef biological systems. Exorbitant supplements can prompt algal excess, covering corals and upsetting their development. Substance contaminations can straightforwardly hurt coral wellbeing and add to coral reef corruption.

5. Preservation Endeavors and Drives

Marine Safeguarded Regions (MPAs)

Laying out Marine Safeguarded Regions (MPAs) is a vital procedure for the preservation of coral reefs. MPAs limit specific human exercises inside characterized regions, giving a shelter where marine life can flourish without the tensions of overfishing and natural surroundings debasement. Very much oversaw MPAs add to the flexibility of coral reef biological systems and backing research endeavors to more readily grasp these intricate conditions.

Supportable Fisheries The executives

Advancing supportable fisheries the executives is fundamental for the drawn out strength of coral reefs. Carrying out guidelines that breaking point fishing pressure, safeguard weak species, and forestall disastrous fishing rehearses adds to the protection of biodiversity. Local area based administration approaches include nearby partners in dynamic cycles, encouraging a feeling of pride and obligation.

Lessening Spillover and Contamination

Endeavors to lessen contamination and spillover from land-based sources are pivotal for coral reef protection. Carrying out accepted procedures in horticulture, wastewater treatment, and metropolitan arranging can limit the presentation of hurtful supplements and synthetic substances into marine conditions. Public mindfulness missions and training drives assume a part in empowering capable ecological practices.

Environmental Change Alleviation

Tending to the underlying drivers of environmental change, especially the decrease of ozone harming substance outflows, is central to the protection of coral reefs. Worldwide drives to moderate environmental change add to the versatility of coral reef biological systems by decreasing the stressors related with climbing ocean temperatures and sea fermentation.

6. Future Points of view and Exploration Bearings

Versatility and Variation

Research zeroed in on understanding the versatility and variation of coral reefs is basic for their drawn out endurance. Researchers are examining the components that permit specific corals to endure higher temperatures and investigating the potential for helped advancement to upgrade the strength of coral populaces.

Mechanical Arrangements

Progressions in innovation, like remote detecting and submerged mechanical technology, give significant apparatuses to observing and concentrating on coral reefs. These advances empower researchers to survey reef wellbeing, recognize stressors, and execute designated preservation mediations. Remote detecting, specifically, takes into consideration huge scope checking of coral reef environments after some time.

Local area Commitment and Instruction

Local area commitment and training drives are fundamental for the outcome of coral reef preservation endeavors. Engaging nearby networks with information about the worth of coral reefs, supportable practices, and the significance of biodiversity cultivates a feeling of stewardship.

Connected with networks are bound to take part in preservation exercises and backing drives that safeguard coral reef biological systems.

2.3 Popularization of Clownfish through Media and Film

The promotion of clownfish through media and film plays had a urgent impact in lifting these energetic marine animals to notable status in mainstream society. One of the vital impetuses for their far reaching acknowledgment was the enlivened film "Tracking down Nemo," delivered by Pixar Liveliness Studios in 2003. The film highlighted the charming person Nemo, a youthful clownfish, on a dazzling excursion through the limitlessness of the sea. The enchanting depiction of clownfish in the film, with their particular markings and special ways of behaving, caught the hearts of crowds worldwide.

The progress of "Tracking down Nemo" made clownfish commonly recognized names as well as started a flood of interest in marine life and reef biological systems. The film's depiction of the harmonious connection among clownfish and ocean anemones, as well as the difficulties they face in the sea, added to a more noteworthy familiarity with marine protection issues.

Following the progress of "Tracking down Nemo," its spin-off, "Tracking down Dory," proceeded to feature the appeal and allure of clownfish. These movies have left a persevering through influence, rousing instructive drives, aquarium displays, and in any event, impacting customer decisions in the aquarium exchange.

Past enlivened highlights, narratives and nature programs further add to the advancement of clownfish. By offering looks into their normal ways of behaving, complex biological systems, and the sensitive equilibrium of marine life, media has turned into an amazing asset for cultivating appreciation and comprehension of clownfish among crowds, all things considered.

Fundamentally, the promotion of clownfish through media and film has engaged as well as instructed, encouraging a feeling of marvel and obligation toward the submerged world and its entrancing occupants.

Chapter 3

Nemo's Legacy: Clownfish In Virtual Oceans

The permanent appeal of clownfish, advocated by the enlivened film "Tracking down Nemo," rises above the bounds of the cinema and reaches out into the virtual domain of gaming. Nemo's Inheritance alludes to the persevering through effect of these lively marine characters on the universe of virtual seas inside gaming conditions. This investigation digs into the crossing point of clownfish and virtual universes, analyzing their portrayal, jobs, and the more extensive ramifications for gaming devotees and marine protection.

II. The Development of Clownfish in Gaming

From Pixels to Lively Authenticity

The portrayal of clownfish in gaming has gone through a surprising development, reflecting progressions in innovation and the mission forever vivid encounters. Early pixelated versions in exemplary games gave approach to additional point by point and sensible depictions as designs capacities extended. Current gaming conditions now exhibit clownfish with staggering visual devotion, catching their unmistakable tinge, ways of behaving, and advantageous associations with ocean anemones.

Impact of Enlivened Movies

The impact of enlivened films like "Tracking down Nemo" is obvious in the gaming business. Designers draw motivation from the charming characters and connecting with accounts, coordinating clownfish into gaming storylines and conditions. The progress of Nemo and his submerged companions has made a social peculiarity, driving interest for gaming encounters that transport players into virtual seas suggestive of the energized film.

III. Clownfish as Playable Characters

Special Capacities and Qualities

In the domain of virtual seas, clownfish frequently rise above the job of simple view or foundation components. Game designers influence the remarkable attributes of clownfish to make drawing in and dynamic interactivity.

From their little size and dexterity to their unmistakable variety evolving capacities, clownfish act as playable characters with characteristics that add an additional layer of system and challenge for gamers.

Investigation and Missions

Clownfish-driven missions and storylines have turned into a staple in gaming stories. Players set out on submerged experiences, exploring through coral reefs, staying away from hunters, and participating in journeys that reflect the difficulties looked by genuine clownfish. These gaming encounters engage as well as instruct players about the complexities of marine life and the significance of safeguarding submerged biological systems.

IV. Advantageous Connections and Virtual Nature

Virtual Biological systems and Ecological Elements

The coordination of clownfish into virtual biological systems stretches out past their singular attributes. Game engineers endeavor to imitate the intricacy of certifiable coral reefs by consolidating advantageous associations with ocean anemones and other marine species. Virtual seas become dynamic conditions where players witness the interchange of biological connections, cultivating a more profound appreciation for the sensitive equilibrium of marine environments.

Effect of Player Decisions on Virtual Conditions

A vital part of clownfish in virtual seas is the joining of player decisions that influence the in-game climate. Players might be entrusted with protection missions, pursuing choices that influence the strength of the virtual reef. These decisions add to a feeling of natural stewardship, resembling genuine endeavors to protect coral reefs and marine life.

V. Instructive Importance and Preservation Informing

Learning Through Play

Clownfish in virtual seas act as instructive apparatuses, offering players an intelligent and engaging method for finding out about sea life science and protection. Gamified components, for example, tests, data pop-ups, and intuitive difficulties, upgrade players' information about clownfish ways of behaving, their parts in coral reef environments, and the more extensive difficulties confronting sea protection.

Preservation Informing in Gaming Stories

Consolidating preservation stories inside gaming storylines has turned into a strong technique for bringing issues to light about certifiable issues. Virtual seas highlighting clownfish frequently incorporate plotlines focused on ecological dangers like coral dying, overfishing, and contamination.

Through vivid narrating, gamers are sharpened to the delicacy of marine environments, encouraging a feeling of obligation for the prosperity of virtual and genuine seas the same.

VI. Innovative Progressions and Augmented Reality

Vivid Encounters with Computer generated Reality (VR)

The coming of computer generated reality (VR) has launch clownfish in gaming higher than ever of drenching. VR innovation permits players to plunge into virtual seas, investigating coral reefs as though they were really submerged. The tangible experience of swimming close by clownfish, encompassed by the sights and hints of an energetic virtual biological system, improves the profound association among players and the marine climate.

Artificial intelligence driven Collaborations and Authenticity

Man-made brainpower (computer based intelligence) adds to the authenticity of clownfish ways of behaving inside virtual seas. Computer based intelligence driven characters respond to player activities and natural changes, making a dynamic and responsive gaming experience. This degree of refinement improves ongoing interaction as well as mirrors the potential for innovation to recreate sensible natural connections in virtual conditions.

VII. Social and Social Effect

Worldwide Allure and Social Impact

Clownfish in virtual seas have accomplished worldwide allure, rising above social limits. The impact of enlivened films, especially "Tracking down Nemo," has added to the comprehensiveness of clownfish as adored virtual characters. The social effect reaches out past gaming, impacting stock, web-based entertainment patterns, and, surprisingly, moving genuine drives for marine protection.

Local area Commitment and Mindfulness

Gaming people group, joined by their common encounters in virtual seas, have become stages for conversations on marine protection. Online gatherings, virtual entertainment gatherings, and gaming occasions act as spaces where players trade data, share protection tips, and participate in discoursed about this present reality challenges confronting clownfish and coral reefs.

VIII. Challenges and Moral Contemplations

Overexploitation and Virtual Aquariums

The prevalence of clownfish in virtual seas raises moral contemplations in regards to the potential for overexploitation inside gaming conditions. Virtual aquariums that permit players to gather and exchange virtual marine species may unintentionally sustain a commodification outlook, reflecting genuine worries about the aquarium exchange's effect on wild populaces.

Adjusting Amusement and Preservation Informing

Designers face the test of finding some kind of harmony between making engaging gaming encounters and integrating significant preservation informing. The gamble of natural messages being eclipsed by interactivity mechanics or stories exists, underscoring the requirement for smart plan and coordinated effort with preservation specialists.

IX. Future Patterns and Conceivable outcomes

Intuitive Resident Science Drives

The mix of clownfish into gaming conditions opens opportunities for intelligent resident science drives. Gaming stages could team up with sea life researchers to gather information on player communications, inclinations, and virtual preservation decisions. This information could contribute important bits of knowledge into player discernments and ways of behaving connected with marine preservation.

Cross-stage Network and Preservation Missions

What's in store holds potential for cross-stage network, where gaming encounters rise above individual gadgets. Virtual seas highlighting clownfish could become interconnected center points for worldwide protection crusades. Players from various areas of the planet could team up on virtual preservation projects, reflecting genuine endeavors to address worldwide ecological difficulties.

3.1 Introduction to Virtual Oceans in Gaming

Gaming Past Limits

The development of gaming has risen above traditional limits, welcoming players into vivid advanced scenes that stretch out a long ways past the bounds of the real world. Virtual seas, when a simple scenery in gaming conditions, have developed into complicated, powerful biological systems that enrapture players and proposition an exceptional mix of diversion, training, and investigation.

Mechanical Progressions and Authenticity

Mechanical progressions in illustrations, computerized reasoning, and augmented reality play played vital parts in forming the rise of virtual seas in gaming. Designers currently bridle the force of state of the art innovation to establish amazingly sensible submerged conditions, complete with many-sided environments, various marine life, and dynamic collaborations impacted by player decisions.

II. The Appeal of Virtual Seas

Escape into Strange Profundities

The appeal of virtual seas lies in their capacity to move players to strange profundities and neglected domains. Gamers can lower themselves into the secrets of the profound, swimming close by great marine animals, exploring lively coral reefs, and leaving on journeys that reflect the intricacies of genuine maritime biological systems.

Instructive Potential

Past diversion, virtual seas present an instructive outskirts. Games including practical sea life science, ecological science, and protection stories offer players an amazing chance to find out about the sensitive equilibrium of submerged biological systems. The intelligent idea of gaming changes learning into a dynamic and connecting with experience, encouraging a more profound comprehension of marine life and the difficulties they face.

III. Innovative Groundworks of Virtual Seas

Designs and Authenticity

The visual allure of virtual seas relies on the authenticity accomplished through cutting edge illustrations. High-goal surfaces, many-sided enumerating of marine life, and reasonable lighting impacts add to a vivid gaming experience. The objective is to imitate the lively varieties, different species, and multifaceted environments tracked down in genuine seas, furnishing players with an outwardly staggering and legitimate submerged experience.

Man-made reasoning and Dynamic Conditions

Man-made reasoning (simulated intelligence) is a foundation in the production of dynamic virtual seas. Computer based intelligence calculations administer the ways of behaving of marine life, adjusting to player collaborations and ecological changes. This powerful nature guarantees that the virtual sea is certainly not a static background however a no nonsense environment where marine species show exact reactions to boosts, making a feeling of authenticity and unusualness.

Computer generated Reality (VR) and Vivid Encounters

Computer generated reality (VR) innovation takes the drenching to exceptional levels. Players outfitted with VR headsets can investigate virtual seas in three-layered space, giving an uplifted feeling of presence. The tangible experience of being encircled by amphibian conditions, combined with intelligent controls, enhances the profound association among players and the computerized seascape.

IV. Key Components of Virtual Seas in Gaming

Playable Characters and Marine Symbols

Virtual seas frequently include playable characters that occupy the submerged domains. These characters, going from marine symbols to notable species like clownfish, present an individual and interesting component to the gaming experience. Players can explore the sea profundities, participate in missions, and communicate with other virtual marine life, each with its one of a kind arrangement of difficulties and prizes.

Cooperative Connections and Environmental Elements

To improve authenticity, game engineers consolidate advantageous connections and environmental elements inside virtual seas. The transaction between various species, the impact of ecological elements, and the outcomes of player decisions add to a unique environment. Protection components, like coral blanching or overfishing, might be coordinated into ongoing interaction, featuring the fragile equilibrium of marine conditions.

Submerged Scenes and Focal points

The production of different and outwardly dazzling submerged scenes is significant for a convincing virtual sea. Coral reefs, submerged caves, and deep fields act as focal points, empowering investigation and disclosure. Secret fortunes, interesting species, and submerged milestones add layers of interest to the gaming experience, propelling players to dig further into the virtual profundities.

V. Portrayals of Marine Life in Virtual Seas

Reasonable Portrayals of Species

Headways in designs innovation consider sensible portrayals of marine life in virtual seas. From the effortless developments of dolphins to the mind boggling designs on a seahorse, the meticulousness rejuvenates computerized oceanic species. Players can notice, communicate with, and find out about a different cluster of marine animals, each adding to the legitimacy of the virtual maritime climate.

Playable and Notable Species

Playable species, frequently filling in as symbols for players, differ from normal fish to notable marine creatures like sharks, whales, and dolphins. The consideration of these species adds variety to interactivity as well as features the immense scope of marine life present in certifiable seas. Furthermore, notable species, for example, clownfish or seahorses, convey social importance and add to the general allure of virtual seas.

VI. Gamification of Marine Protection

Protection Missions and Journeys

Virtual seas offer an extraordinary stage for gamifying marine preservation endeavors. Designers integrate protection missions and journeys into ongoing interaction, entrusting players with challenges that reflect genuine ecological dangers. By finishing these missions, players add to the prosperity of the virtual sea and, at times, may open extra satisfied or capacities.

Instructive Targets and Mindfulness

Gamification fills in as a device for bringing issues to light about marine protection issues. Instructive targets, introduced as in-game difficulties or educational pop-ups, furnish players with experiences into the significance of safeguarding seas. This mindfulness reaches out past the virtual domain, cultivating a feeling of ecological obligation among players and empowering informed decisions in reality.

VII. Challenges and Moral Contemplations

Overexploitation and Virtual Aquariums

The gamification of virtual seas presents moral contemplations, especially concerning overexploitation inside gaming conditions. Virtual aquariums, where players can gather and exchange virtual marine species, may inadvertently propagate a commodification mentality like worries about the effect of this present reality aquarium exchange on wild populaces.

Adjusting Diversion and Preservation Informing

Engineers face the test of finding some kind of harmony between making engaging gaming encounters and integrating significant preservation informing. The gamble exists of ecological messages being eclipsed by interactivity mechanics or stories, accentuating the requirement for smart plan that guarantees both commitment and instructive effect.

VIII. Future Patterns and Conceivable outcomes

Intelligent Resident Science Drives

The mix of virtual seas into gaming opens opportunities for intuitive resident science drives. Gaming stages could team up with sea life researchers to gather information on player communications, inclinations, and virtual protection decisions. This information could contribute significant experiences into player discernments and ways of behaving connected with marine protection, possibly supporting genuine logical endeavors.

Cross-stage Availability and Worldwide Missions

What's in store holds potential for cross-stage network, where gaming encounters rise above individual gadgets. Virtual seas including cross-stage network could become interconnected centers for worldwide preservation crusades. Players from various regions of the planet could team up on virtual preservation projects, reflecting genuine endeavors to address worldwide natural difficulties.

3.2 Influence of Marine Life in Game Design

The impact of marine life in game plan stretches out past the simple production of outwardly staggering submerged conditions. It penetrates the actual embodiment of gaming encounters, forming accounts, mechanics, and player cooperations. This investigation dives into the complex manners by which marine life impacts game plan, from the underlying conceptualization of thoughts to the acknowledgment of virtual seas abounding with lively oceanic biological systems.

II. Conceptualization and Motivation

From Nature to Creative mind

The conceptualization of marine-themed games frequently starts with drawing motivation from the mind boggling excellence and variety of the sea. Game originators drench themselves in the investigation of sea life science, investigating the novel ways of behaving, attributes, and biological systems that characterize submerged life. This profound jump into nature fills in as a wellspring of imagination, permitting planners to imagine fantastical universes and species that catch the substance of the sea's marvels.

Notorious Marine Species as Characters

The notorious idea of specific marine species frequently impels them into focal jobs as characters inside game accounts. Animals like dolphins, sharks, and seahorses, with their unmistakable elements and social importance, become heroes, adversaries, or friends in virtual universes. The commonality and allure of these species add to the appeal of game characters, making profound associations among players and the advanced marine domain.

III. Authenticity and Designs

Headways in Practical Illustrations

The constant progressions in illustrations innovation play had a critical impact in rejuvenating marine life inside gaming conditions. High-goal surfaces, many-sided specifying of scales and balances, and reasonable activitys add to a vivid visual encounter. Game originators take a stab at a degree of authenticity that permits players to feel as though they are genuinely lowered in a submerged world, wondering about the excellence of marine species.

Catching Development and Conduct

Realness in game plan includes making exact portrayals of marine species as well as catching their development and conduct. From the smooth skim of a manta beam to the inquisitive tricks of a school of fish, careful thoughtfulness regarding development examples and ways of behaving adds layers of authenticity. This tender loving care upgrades player inundation, making the virtual sea a dynamic and living biological system.

IV. Game Mechanics and Intelligence

Playable Marine Characters

Marine life frequently stretches out past being simple foundation components, developing into playable characters with unmistakable capacities and ways of behaving. Game mechanics might use the one of a kind highlights of marine species, permitting players to explore through difficulties utilizing the dexterity of a dolphin, the disguise capacities of a cuttlefish, or the strength of an incredible white shark. This joining of playable marine characters adds profundity and variety to interactivity encounters.

Harmonious Connections and Environment Elements

To lift the legitimacy of virtual seas, game architects integrate harmonious connections and environment elements into the center mechanics. Players might observer the reliance of various marine species, where the activities of one influence the whole environment. By mimicking the fragile equilibrium of certifiable biological systems, games urge players to think about the more extensive natural ramifications of their in-game decisions.

V. Instructive Components and Ecological Mindfulness

Sea life Science Gamified

Marine-themed games frequently act as gamified instructive apparatuses, giving players chances to find out about sea life science in a drawing in and intelligent way.

Instructive components might incorporate enlightening pop-ups, tests, and difficulties that confer information about various marine species, their parts in environments, and the protection challenges they face. Gaming turns into an entryway to grasping the intricacies of marine life.

Ecological Protection Accounts

Consolidating ecological protection stories inside game storylines is a strong strategy for bringing issues to light about true issues. Players might wind up exploring virtual seas undermined by contamination, overfishing, or environmental change. By drawing in with these difficulties inside the game, players foster a comprehension of the dire requirement for marine preservation and the job they can play in safeguarding virtual and true seas the same.

VI. Social Importance and Portrayal

Iconography and Imagery

Marine life conveys social importance around the world, frequently filling in as images in different social orders. Game fashioners tap into this social supply, integrating marine imagery and iconography into their manifestations. From antiquated fantasies encompassing ocean animals to contemporary relationship with marine protection, these social references enhance the account profundity of marine-themed games.

Variety in Portrayal

The portrayal of marine life in games reaches out to exhibiting the variety of species tracked down in certifiable seas. While notorious species like dolphins and sharks hold social noticeable quality, game originators additionally feature less popular species, advancing a more comprehensive and exact depiction of marine biodiversity. This variety in portrayal adds to the instructive worth of games, acquainting players with the immense range of submerged life.

VII. Challenges and Moral Contemplations

Morals of Virtual Aquariums

The incorporation of virtual aquariums inside games raises moral contemplations connected with the possible commodification of virtual marine species. Players might can gather, exchange, or take advantage of advanced portrayals of marine life, repeating worries about the effect of this present reality aquarium exchange on wild populaces. Finding some kind of harmony among diversion and moral contemplations turns into a urgent part of game plan.

Adjusting Protection Informing

Game fashioners face the test of adjusting preservation informing inside the setting of diversion. While the gamification of ecological difficulties is a significant device for bringing issues to light, there is a gamble that protection messages might be eclipsed by ongoing interaction mechanics. Smart plan and cooperation with preservation specialists are fundamental to guarantee that games successfully convey both diversion and protection stories.

VIII. Future Patterns and Potential outcomes

Headways in Computer generated Experience (VR)

The eventual fate of marine life in game plan holds energizing prospects with progressions in augmented simulation (VR) innovation. VR gives an unrivaled degree of drenching, permitting players to investigate virtual seas in three-layered space. The tangible experience of wearing VR headsets and being encircled by submerged conditions improves the profound association among players and the advanced marine domain.

Intuitive Resident Science Drives

The coordination of marine life into gaming conditions opens opportunities for intuitive resident science drives. Game stages could team up with sea life researchers to gather information on player connections, inclinations, and virtual protection decisions. This information could contribute important bits of knowledge into player insights and ways of behaving connected with marine preservation, possibly helping certifiable logical endeavors.

3.3 Iconic Representation of Clownfish in Virtual Worlds

The notorious portrayal of clownfish in virtual universes has become inseparable from the appeal and charm of submerged gaming encounters. From the pixelated domains of exemplary games to the incredibly sensible conditions of current virtual seas, clownfish have risen above their seagoing environments to become cherished images inside the gaming scene.

This investigation dives into the development of the notable portrayal of clownfish in virtual universes, following their excursion from early pixels to the energetic authenticity of contemporary gaming conditions.

II. Early Pixels: The Coming of Clownfish in Exemplary Games

Pixelated Trailblazers

In the beginning of gaming, when designs were restricted to pixels and restricted variety ranges, clownfish made their presentation as spearheading amphibian characters. Exemplary games highlighting submerged experiences frequently included improved on portrayals of clownfish, conspicuous by their particular orange and white tinge.

While ailing in many-sided subtleties, these pixelated versions established the groundwork for the famous status that clownfish would later accomplish in virtual universes.

Imagery of Variety and Structure

The utilization of lively tones and unmistakable structures in pixelated clownfish filled a double need. On one hand, it considered simple visual acknowledgment in the frequently restricted graphical constancy of early games. Then again, the imagery of these varieties reflected this present reality excellence of clownfish, making them stand apart in the midst of the advanced waves. This early portrayal set up for the persevering through relationship among clownfish and submerged gaming undertakings.

III. Headways in Illustrations: Authenticity Becomes the dominant focal point

From 2D to 3D Authenticity

As gaming innovation progressed, taking the jump from 2D to 3D designs, clownfish went through a change in their virtual portrayal. The reception of three-layered demonstrating took into consideration a more practical portrayal of clownfish, complete with itemized surfaces, liquid livelinesss, and nuanced developments. This shift denoted a vital second in the notorious portrayal of clownfish, as players could now observe these virtual animals in an outwardly staggering and vivid way.

Scrupulousness and Conduct

The notorious portrayal of clownfish in virtual universes developed to incorporate an uplifted degree of tender loving care. Game fashioners started integrating the extraordinary ways of behaving and qualities of clownfish into their virtual partners. From the many-sided examples of their balances to the manner in which they cooperated with virtual conditions, these subtleties added to a more legitimate and drawing in portrayal of clownfish inside gaming environments.

IV. Playable Characters: Clownfish as Virtual Symbols

Unmistakable Capacities and Characteristics

Clownfish rose above the job of simple foundation components, becoming the overwhelming focus as playable characters inside virtual seas. Game engineers utilized the particular capacities and characteristics of clownfish to make drawing in interactivity encounters. The little size and nimbleness of clownfish, joined with their capacity to explore through coral reefs and collaborate with other marine life, acquainted another aspect with gaming undertakings. Players could now encapsulate the energetic soul of clownfish as they explored virtual submerged universes.

Harmonious Connections and Missions

The notorious portrayal of clownfish reached out past their singular attributes to incorporate advantageous associations with virtual ocean anemones. Missions and storylines frequently rotated around the exceptional connection among clownfish and ocean anemones, reflecting this present reality environmental organization. Players wound up setting out on journeys that investigated the difficulties and undertakings looked by these famous marine animals, further establishing the social meaning of clownfish in virtual universes.

V. Innovative Progressions: Augmented Reality and Then some

Vivid Encounters with Computer generated Reality (VR)

The approach of augmented reality (VR) innovation raised the famous portrayal of clownfish to exceptional degrees of drenching. VR headsets permitted players to jump into virtual seas, encountering the submerged domain in three-layered space. The tactile experience of swimming close by clownfish, encompassed by the sights and hints of a dynamic virtual environment, upgraded the profound association among players and these notable marine characters.

Computer based intelligence driven Cooperations and Authenticity

Computerized reasoning (man-made intelligence) assumed a significant part in improving the authenticity of clownfish ways of behaving inside virtual universes. Computer based intelligence driven characters responded to player activities and natural changes, making a dynamic and responsive gaming experience. The collaborations between virtual clownfish and their environmental factors turned out to be more nuanced, adding to the genuineness of the submerged biological systems. This degree of complexity mirrored the potential for innovation to reenact reasonable natural cooperations in virtual conditions.

VI. Instructive Importance and Protection Informing

Learning Through Play

The notorious portrayal of clownfish in virtual universes has taken on instructive importance, offering players an intelligent and engaging method for finding out about sea life science and preservation. Gamified components, for example, tests, data pop-ups, and intelligent difficulties, improve players' information about clownfish ways of behaving, their parts in coral reef environments, and the more extensive difficulties confronting sea preservation. Gaming turns into a stage for casual schooling, where players retain data while submerged in virtual submerged undertakings.

Protection Informing in Gaming Stories

Consolidating protection accounts inside gaming storylines has turned into a strong technique for bringing issues to light about certifiable natural issues. Virtual seas highlighting clownfish frequently incorporate plotlines fixated on natural dangers like coral blanching, overfishing, and contamination. Through vivid narrating, gamers are sharpened to the delicacy of marine biological systems, cultivating a feeling of obligation for the prosperity of clownfish and their submerged territories.

VII. Social and Social Effect

Worldwide Allure and Social Impact

The notable portrayal of clownfish in virtual universes has accomplished worldwide allure, rising above social limits. The impact of enlivened films, especially "Tracking down Nemo," has added to the all inclusiveness of clownfish as darling virtual characters. The social effect stretches out past gaming, impacting stock, web-based entertainment patterns, and, surprisingly, rousing true drives for marine preservation.

Local area Commitment and Mindfulness

Gaming people group, joined by their common encounters in virtual seas, have become stages for conversations on marine protection. Online discussions, web-based entertainment gatherings, and gaming occasions act as spaces where players trade data, share protection tips, and participate in discoursed about this present reality challenges confronting clownfish and coral reefs. The notable portrayal of clownfish turns into an impetus for local area commitment and mindfulness building.

VIII. Challenges and Moral Contemplations

Overexploitation and Virtual Aquariums

The ubiquity of clownfish in virtual universes raises moral contemplations in regards to the potential for overexploitation inside gaming conditions. Virtual aquariums that permit players to gather and exchange virtual marine species may incidentally propagate a commodification mentality, reflecting genuine worries about the effect of the aquarium exchange on wild populaces. Adjusting the longing for drawing in interactivity with moral contemplations turns into a test for game creators.

Adjusting Amusement and Protection Informing

Designers face the test of finding some kind of harmony between making engaging gaming encounters and consolidating significant protection informing. The gamble of natural messages being eclipsed by ongoing interaction mechanics or accounts exists, accentuating the requirement for smart plan and joint effort with protection specialists. Finding some kind of harmony is pivotal to guaranteeing that gaming encounters enthrall players as well as motivate genuine activity for marine preservation.

IX. Future Patterns and Potential outcomes

Intelligent Resident Science Drives

The mix of clownfish into gaming conditions opens opportunities for intelligent resident science drives. Gaming stages could team up with sea life researchers to gather information on player communications, inclinations, and virtual preservation decisions. This information could contribute significant experiences into player insights and ways of behaving connected with marine preservation, possibly supporting true logical endeavors.

Cross-stage Availability and Preservation Missions

What's in store holds potential for cross-stage availability, where gaming encounters rise above individual gadgets. Virtual seas highlighting clownfish could become interconnected center points for worldwide protection crusades. Players from various areas of the planet could team up on virtual protection projects, reflecting true endeavors to address worldwide natural difficulties.

Chapter 4

Clownfish As Characters And Companions

The captivating universe of gaming has seen the ascent of different characters, each carrying novel characteristics and appeal to virtual undertakings. Among these, clownfish stand apart as notorious characters and partners, rising above their certifiable territories to become dearest elements inside advanced domains. This investigation digs into the complex jobs of clownfish in gaming, from their depiction as playable characters to the charming partners that go with players on virtual excursions.

II. Playable Characters: Clownfish Becoming the dominant focal point
From Pixels to Energetic Authenticity

The excursion of clownfish as playable characters in gaming has developed fundamentally, reflecting the headways in designs and innovation. In the beginning of gaming, clownfish made their pixelated appearances, frequently as heroes exploring through oversimplified submerged scenes. As innovation advanced, their portrayal changed into fun loving authenticity, with multifaceted subtleties, dynamic tones, and similar ways of behaving upgrading their presence in virtual seas.

Unmistakable Characteristics and Capacities

Clownfish, as playable characters, carry with them a bunch of unmistakable characteristics and capacities that put them aside inside gaming biological systems. The little size and spryness of clownfish make them proficient at exploring unpredictable submerged conditions, winding through coral reefs, and getting away from possible dangers. Game engineers influence these qualities to make connecting with interactivity encounters, frequently integrating the special highlights of clownfish to upgrade the general gaming experience.

Investigation and Journeys

The consideration of clownfish as playable characters frequently remains inseparable with submerged investigation and journeys. Players end up setting out on virtual experiences that reflect the difficulties looked by genuine clownfish.

Exploring through coral reefs, staying away from hunters, and taking part in journeys that feature the cooperative connection among clownfish and ocean anemones become focal components of gaming accounts. The intelligent idea of these journeys extends the player's association with clownfish as characters.

III. Cooperative Connections: Clownfish and Ocean Anemones

Copying Certifiable Advantageous interaction

One of the unmistakable parts of clownfish in gaming is the imitating of their genuine harmonious relationship with ocean anemones. In virtual seas, players frequently experience situations where clownfish look for shelter inside the limbs of ocean anemones, tracking down both security and a home. This harmonious bond isn't simply a visual display however turns into a fundamental piece of interactivity, with players exploring difficulties and riddles revolved around the one of a kind association among clownfish and ocean anemones.

Dynamic Collaborations and Interactivity Mechanics

Game designers go past static depictions, presenting dynamic connections and interactivity mechanics that mirror the complexities of the clownfish-ocean anemone relationship. Players might have to decisively use this beneficial interaction to defeat hindrances, open new regions, or even for the purpose of safeguard against virtual hunters. The consolidation of these powerful components upgrades the general gaming experience, offering both diversion and a more profound comprehension of marine biological systems.

IV. Clownfish as Friends: Charming Companions in Virtual Excursions

Close to home Association and Connection

Notwithstanding their jobs as playable characters, clownfish frequently act as charming sidekicks that go with players all through virtual excursions. The profound association among players and their virtual clownfish mates adds a layer of profundity to gaming encounters. These advanced companions, with their lively tricks and particular characters, become something beyond characters — they become colleagues that players become connected to throughout their undertakings.

Customization and Personalization

The capacity to alter and customize virtual clownfish buddies further improves the player's feeling of association. From picking interesting variety examples to choosing individual qualities or ways of behaving, players have the chance to shape their virtual allies to line up with their inclinations. This customization not just adds an individual touch to the gaming experience yet in addition fortifies the connection among players and their clownfish mates.

V. Authenticity and simulated intelligence driven Ways of behaving

Headways in Reasonable Portrayals

The notorious portrayal of clownfish as characters and mates benefits altogether from progressions in illustrations and liveliness advancements. Reasonable portrayals of clownfish, complete with perplexing subtleties like variety varieties, blade developments, and similar ways of behaving, add to an elevated feeling of inundation. The objective is to make virtual clownfish that intently reflect their true partners, permitting players to see the value in the magnificence and intricacy of these marine animals.

Artificial intelligence driven Ways of behaving for Exact Collaboration

Man-made brainpower (simulated intelligence) assumes a critical part in saturating virtual clownfish with similar ways of behaving and connections. Man-made intelligence calculations oversee how these advanced colleagues answer player activities, natural changes, and the general movement of the game. The unique idea of computer based intelligence driven ways of behaving guarantees that clownfish colleagues adjust to various circumstances, cultivating a more vivid and responsive virtual experience.

VI. Instructive Importance: Learning Through Clownfish Partners

Gamified Growth opportunities

The presence of clownfish as partners inside gaming conditions stretches out past amusement, offering gamified opportunities for growth. Players draw in with instructive components flawlessly woven into interactivity, giving data about clownfish science, ways of behaving, and their job in marine biological systems. These gamified opportunities for growth transform virtual excursions into open doors for players to gain information about marine life in an intelligent and pleasant way.

Preservation Informing Through Colleagues

Clownfish associates become courses for protection informing inside gaming stories. Players might experience situations that bring issues to light about certifiable dangers to marine conditions, like coral blanching or overfishing. The consideration of preservation components in the storyline, combined with the profound association players have with their virtual partners, enhances the effect of protection informing and supports a feeling of natural obligation.

VII. Challenges and Moral Contemplations

Adjusting Authenticity and Amusement

Game designers face the continuous test of offsetting authenticity with diversion while depicting clownfish as characters and buddies. While authenticity upgrades the vivid nature of gaming encounters, it should be painstakingly adjusted to try not to overpower players with an excessive amount of detail.

Finding some kind of harmony guarantees that the instructive and protection parts of clownfish portrayal don't eclipse the essential objective of giving a connecting with and agreeable gaming experience.

Moral Contemplations in Virtual Aquariums

The incorporation of virtual aquariums inside gaming conditions raises moral contemplations in regards to the expected commodification of virtual marine species. Players might can gather and exchange virtual clownfish, reflecting worries about the effect of this present reality aquarium exchange on wild populaces. Game designers should explore the moral ramifications of virtual aquariums to forestall accidental adverse results on player insights and certifiable protection perspectives.

VIII. Future Patterns and Potential outcomes

Progressions in Augmented Experience (VR)

What's in store holds energizing opportunities for the portrayal of clownfish in virtual conditions, especially with progressions in augmented experience (VR) innovation. VR gives an unmatched degree of submersion, permitting players to encounter the submerged world close by their clownfish buddies in three-layered space. The tangible lavishness of VR upgrades the close to home association among players and their virtual partners, making a more significant and drawing in gaming experience.

Intuitive Resident Science Drives

The joining of clownfish as characters and mates opens opportunities for intuitive resident science drives. Gaming stages could team up with sea life researchers to gather information on player associations, inclinations, and virtual protection decisions. This information could contribute significant bits of knowledge into player insights and ways of behaving connected with marine preservation, possibly supporting genuine logical endeavors.

4.1 Clownfish as Playable Characters

In the immense and vivid scene of gaming, certain characters stand apart for their appeal, versatility, and fun loving nature. Among these, clownfish have arisen as famous playable characters, enrapturing players with their unmistakable appearance and interesting characteristics. This investigation dives into the diverse job of clownfish as playable characters in gaming, following their development from early pixels to the dynamic, practical elements that presently explore virtual seas.

II. Early Pixels: The Modest Starting points of Clownfish in Gaming

Pixelated Trailblazers

The excursion of clownfish as playable characters can be followed back to the beginning of gaming when illustrations were restricted to pixels and restricted variety ranges. In these pixelated experiences, clownfish made their unassuming presentation, frequently as heroes exploring over-simplified submerged scenes. Regardless of the restrictions of early innovation, the energetic tones and particular examples of clownfish became unmistakable, establishing the groundwork for their getting through presence in gaming domains.

Imagery of Variety and Structure

The utilization of striking tones and particular structures in pixelated clownfish filled both useful and tasteful needs. Past the specialized imperatives of early designs, the imagery of these tones reflected this present reality magnificence of clownfish. Their particular orange and white hue made them outwardly engaging as well as added to their acknowledgment as notable submerged characters, making way for their development in gamed.

III. Progressions in Illustrations: From 2D to 3D Authenticity

Advancement of Authenticity

As gaming innovation advanced, taking the jump from two-layered (2D) to three-layered (3D) illustrations, clownfish went through an extraordinary development. The reception of 3D demonstrating took into consideration a more reasonable portrayal of these sea-going characters. High-goal surfaces, complicated itemizing of scales, and liquid activitys rejuvenated clownfish in manners that were unrealistic in the pixelated period. This change denoted a huge achievement, as clownfish turned out to be more than emblematic portrayals; they developed into dynamic, reasonable substances inside virtual seas.

Meticulousness and Conduct

The headway in illustrations innovation welcomed with it an expanded concentrate to detail and conduct. Game designers looked to catch the substance of clownfish in appearance as well as in the manner in which they moved and communicated with their virtual surroundings. From the smooth influencing of their blades to their particular swimming examples, the thoughtfulness regarding these nuanced ways of behaving added to the legitimacy of clownfish as playable characters, improving the general gaming experience.

IV. Particular Characteristics and Capacities of Clownfish

Little Size, Huge Experiences

Clownfish, as playable characters, bring a bunch of particular characteristics and capacities that put them aside in the gaming scene. Their little size turns into a benefit, permitting players to explore through many-sided submerged conditions easily. The spryness of clownfish, combined with their lively swimming style, acquaints a unique component with interactivity. Whether dashing through coral reefs or investigating stowed away caverns, the minimal size of clownfish opens up interesting opportunities for connecting with undertakings.

Disguise and Endurance Strategies

Integrating true attributes into ongoing interaction, clownfish frequently have remarkable capacities like disguise. Players might wind up exploring virtual seas where clownfish can conceal inside coral developments or mix consistently with their environmental elements. These endurance strategies become fundamental to ongoing interaction, introducing provokes and key open doors for players to investigate.

V. Missions and Experiences: Exploring Difficulties with Clownfish

Submerged Missions

The consideration of clownfish as playable characters frequently remains inseparable with submerged journeys and experiences. Players leave on virtual excursions that reflect the difficulties looked by genuine clownfish. These journeys might include exploring through coral reefs, staying away from hunters, or participating in undertakings that feature the harmonious connection among clownfish and ocean anemones. The powerful idea of submerged missions upgrades the player's association with clownfish as characters, transforming ongoing interaction into a progression of vivid undertakings.

Advantageous Connections and Intelligent Stories

An outstanding part of clownfish as playable characters is the incorporation of cooperative connections into intelligent stories. Game engineers influence the interesting connection among clownfish and ocean anemones, making situations where players should explore difficulties while keeping up with this critical relationship. The intuitive idea of these stories extends the's comprehension player might interpret marine biological systems and cultivates a feeling of obligation for the prosperity of their virtual clownfish mates.

VI. Innovative Headways: Computer generated Reality (VR) and Man-made consciousness (simulated intelligence)

Vivid Encounters with Augmented Reality

The appearance of computer generated reality (VR) innovation has taken the experience of playing clownfish characters to exceptional degrees of inundation. VR headsets permit players to plunge into virtual seas, encountering the submerged world in three-layered space. The tangible wealth of VR, combined with the capacity to cooperate with the virtual climate in a more natural manner, improves the close to home association among players and their clownfish symbols.

Computer based intelligence driven Ways of behaving for Authenticity

Man-made consciousness (computer based intelligence) assumes a urgent part in upgrading the authenticity of clownfish ways of behaving inside virtual seas. Computer based intelligence driven calculations administer how these advanced characters answer player activities, ecological changes, and the general movement of the game. The unique idea of man-made intelligence driven ways of behaving guarantees that clownfish symbols adjust to various circumstances, making a more vivid and responsive virtual experience.

VII. Instructive Importance: Learning Through Clownfish Characters

Gamified Opportunities for growth

Clownfish characters inside gaming conditions act as conductors for gamified growth opportunities. Players draw in with instructive components consistently woven into interactivity, giving data about clownfish science, ways of behaving, and their job in marine environments. These gamified opportunities for growth transform virtual experiences into valuable open doors for players to gain information about marine life in an intuitive and charming way.

Protection Informing Through Interactivity

The presence of clownfish characters likewise opens roads for integrating preservation informing inside gaming stories. Players might experience situations that bring issues to light about genuine dangers to marine conditions, like coral fading or overfishing. The consideration of preservation components in the storyline, combined with the vivid idea of interactivity, enhances the effect of protection informing and supports a feeling of ecological obligation.

VIII. Challenges and Moral Contemplations

Adjusting Authenticity and Diversion

Game engineers face the continuous test of offsetting authenticity with diversion while depicting clownfish as playable characters. While authenticity improves the vivid nature of gaming encounters, it should be painstakingly adjusted to try not to overpower players with an excessive amount of detail. Finding some kind of harmony guarantees that the instructive and preservation parts of clownfish portrayal don't eclipse the essential objective of giving a drawing in and pleasant gaming experience.

Moral Contemplations in Virtual Aquariums

The incorporation of virtual aquariums inside gaming conditions raises moral contemplations with respect to the possible commodification of virtual marine species. Players might can gather and exchange virtual clownfish, reflecting worries about the effect of this present reality aquarium exchange on wild populaces. Game engineers should explore the moral ramifications of virtual aquariums to forestall accidental unfortunate results on player insights and certifiable protection mentalities.

IX. Future Patterns and Potential outcomes

Intuitive Resident Science Drives

The coordination of clownfish as playable characters opens opportunities for intelligent resident science drives. Gaming stages could team up with sea life researchers to gather information on player cooperations, inclinations, and virtual preservation decisions. This information could contribute significant experiences into player discernments and ways of behaving connected with marine protection, possibly supporting certifiable logical endeavors.

Progressions in Expanded Reality (AR)

What's in store holds energizing prospects with progressions in expanded reality (AR). AR overlays computerized components onto this present reality climate, offering an extraordinary mix of virtual and actual encounters. Players might actually cooperate with clownfish characters in certifiable settings, bringing the enchantment of virtual seas into the daily existences of players.

4.2 Role of Clownfish in Storytelling

Narrating, a well established custom, has developed to envelop different mediums, and inside the huge embroidery of stories, the clownfish has arisen as an enamoring hero. From antiquated fantasies to present day computerized narrating, these lively marine animals have assumed different and emblematic parts. This investigation dives into the complex job of clownfish in narrating, disentangling their importance in social accounts, writing, and advanced domains.

II. Mythic Beginnings: Clownfish in Social Stories

Maritime Legends and Imagery

The sea, a domain of secret and miracle, has been a rich wellspring of motivation for fantasies across societies. Clownfish end up woven into the texture of these fantasies, representing strength, flexibility, and the interconnectedness of marine life. In certain societies, they are depicted as couriers of the ocean divine beings, while in others, their lively varieties represent karma and thriving. These mythic beginnings lay the basis for the persevering through imagery of clownfish in social narrating.

Epitomizing Submerged Spirits

Clownfish, with their striking appearance and extraordinary ways of behaving, frequently assume the job of submerged spirits or enchanted creatures in social stories. Their capacity to explore the multifaceted biological systems of coral reefs turns into an illustration for crossing the intricacies of life's difficulties. These mythic depictions add to the social meaning of clownfish, raising them from simple marine animals to notorious images in narrating.

III. Abstract Imagery: Clownfish in Writing

Analogies of Tirelessness and Boldness

Writing, an impression of human encounters, consolidates clownfish as similitudes for tirelessness and boldness. Stories highlighting clownfish heroes frequently investigate topics of strength notwithstanding misfortune. The intrinsic difficulties of submerged life, for example, exploring through coral reefs and confronting hunters, become purposeful anecdotes for life's obstructions. The excursion of clownfish characters reflects the all inclusive human experience of defeating difficulties sincerely and fortitude.

Family Bonds and Sustaining Senses

Clownfish, known for their exceptional family structure and the supporting job of guys in raising posterity, become images of familial bonds in writing. Stories that feature the defensive senses of clownfish guardians reverberate with subjects of affection, penance, and the rugged ties that tight spot families together. These abstract depictions add to the charming picture of clownfish as mindful and given guardians, adding profundity to their part in narrating.

IV. Enlivened Experiences: Clownfish in Film and TV

Tracking down Nemo and Then some

The vivified film "Tracking down Nemo" slung clownfish into the spotlight, acquainting them with a worldwide crowd in an endearing story. Marlin, the overprotective dad, leaves on a dangerous excursion across the sea to track down his child, Nemo.

This true to life work of art engaged crowds as well as brought clownfish into the domain of mainstream society. The outcome of "Tracking down Nemo" made ready for clownfish to become notable characters in enlivened narrating.

Humanoid attribution and Profound Reverberation

The human depiction of clownfish characters in vivified narrating charms them to crowds, everything being equal. By permeating these marine animals with human-like feelings, characters, and engaging battles, narrators make accounts that resound inwardly. Whether confronting difficulties, framing improbable companionships, or leaving on legendary undertakings, clownfish characters summon compassion and association, cultivating a more profound commitment with the narrating experience.

V. Computerized Domains: Clownfish in Computer games

Playable Heroes

The computerized age introduced another period for narrating, with computer games becoming vivid stages for account investigation. Clownfish, with their energetic varieties and unmistakable attributes, changed from uninvolved characters to playable heroes. Computer games including clownfish as focal characters welcome players to step into the balances of these marine animals, exploring virtual seas, tackling difficulties, and leaving on journeys that reflect their genuine ways of behaving.

Advantageous Stories and Virtual Biological systems

In advanced narrating, clownfish frequently end up in advantageous stories inside virtual biological systems. Players explore the difficulties of submerged conditions, shaping collusions with virtual ocean anemones, and encountering the interconnectedness of marine life. The unique idea of these accounts reflects this present reality beneficial interaction among clownfish and ocean anemones, upgrading the narrating experience by coordinating environmental topics.

VI. Instructive Importance: Clownfish as Narrating Diplomats

Gamified Opportunities for growth

Past diversion, clownfish assume a urgent part in gamified opportunities for growth inside computerized narrating. Instructive computer games influence the allure of clownfish characters to confer information about sea life science, coral reefs, and protection. Players, while participated in intelligent narrating, assimilate data about this present reality partners of their virtual friends, changing the gaming experience into an instructive excursion.

Protection Informing in Advanced Stories

Computerized narrating including clownfish turns into an incredible asset for preservation informing. Games with ecological subjects bring issues to light about the difficulties confronting marine environments, like coral blanching and living space annihilation. The close to home association fashioned among players and their virtual clownfish colleagues fills in as a course for passing on true preservation messages. Through computerized stories, clownfish become envoys for marine protection, moving a feeling of obligation for the seas.

VII. Social and Social Effect

Worldwide Allure and Social Impact

The social and social effect of clownfish in narrating reaches out past individual accounts. The worldwide progress of energized movies and computer games highlighting clownfish characters has added to their social impact. Clownfish, once restricted to maritime legends, have become unmistakable images in mainstream society, impacting stock, virtual entertainment patterns, and, surprisingly, moving certifiable drives for marine preservation.

Local area Commitment and Shared Accounts

Clownfish stories cultivate local area commitment as crowds interface through shared accounts. Online gatherings, web-based entertainment gatherings, and fan networks become spaces where people trade considerations, share encounters, and express their liking for clownfish characters. The common love for these marine animals rises above topographical limits, making a worldwide local area joincd by the tales of these submerged heroes.

VIII. Challenges and Moral Contemplations

Adjusting Amusement and Preservation Informing

Narrators face the test of offsetting amusement with preservation informing, especially in advanced stories. While the vivid idea of narrating in computer games and energized films enraptures crowds, there is a need to guarantee that protection messages are really passed on without eclipsing the essential objective of diversion. Finding some kind of harmony is vital to cultivating ecological mindfulness without compromising the narrating experience.

Moral Contemplations in Promotion

The fame of clownfish in narrating, particularly in enlivened movies and computer games, raises moral contemplations. The gamble of overexploitation, driven by the interest for virtual portrayals of marine species, matches genuine worries about the effect of advocacy on wild populaces.

Narrators and designers should explore these moral contemplations, guaranteeing that the ubiquity of clownfish characters doesn't accidentally add to unfortunate results for their genuine partners.

IX. Future Patterns and Conceivable outcomes

Intelligent Virtual Encounters

What's to come holds invigorating opportunities for intuitive virtual encounters that rise above conventional narrating mediums. Computer generated reality (VR) and expanded reality (AR) advancements offer vivid stages where clients can draw in with clownfish characters in exceptional ways. The tactile wealth of VR and the mixing of virtual and true components in AR present open doors for narrating encounters that go past the limits of screens.

Proceeded with Reconciliation into Protection Drives

Clownfish characters are probably going to proceed with their reconciliation into preservation drives through narrating. Future accounts might dig further into genuine ecological difficulties, empowering players and crowds to take part in protection endeavors effectively. The convergence of narrating, gaming, and ecological backing could prompt creative methodologies for tending to marine protection issues.

4.3 Emotional Connections with Virtual Marine Life

In the steadily extending domain of computerized encounters, the association among people and virtual marine life has risen above simple diversion. From the alleviating profundities of virtual seas to the lively coral reefs of gaming scenes, people are manufacturing personal securities with computerized portrayals of marine life. This investigation dives into the significant close to home associations that clients lay out with virtual marine life, investigating the variables adding to this peculiarity and its more extensive ramifications.

II. The Ascent of Virtual Marine Life

Advancement of Computerized Authenticity

Progressions in innovation have changed the depiction of marine life in computerized domains. From early pixelated portrayals to the ongoing time of superior quality illustrations and vivid computer generated simulation encounters, the development of advanced authenticity plays had a vital impact in encouraging close to home associations. Clients presently experience virtual marine existence with similar developments, unpredictable subtleties, and ways of behaving that intently reflect their certifiable partners, improving the general feeling of drenching.

Humanoid attribution in Computerized Stories

Humanoid attribution, the attribution of human-like characteristics to non-human substances, is a critical component in laying out close to home associations with virtual marine life. In computerized stories, marine animals are frequently supplied with characters, feelings, and appealing ways of behaving. This human focal point permits clients to extend human feelings onto virtual marine characters, cultivating a feeling of compassion and association.

III. Factors Adding to Close to home Associations

Visual Authenticity and Style

The visual authenticity and style of virtual marine life contribute fundamentally to the close to home effect of advanced encounters. Top notch designs, lively varieties, and meticulousness establish outwardly dazzling portrayals of marine conditions. Clients wind up enamored by the magnificence of virtual coral reefs, the effortless developments of fish, and the unique biological systems that unfurl before their eyes. This visual allure turns into an impetus for close to home commitment.

Intuitive Ways of behaving and Responsiveness

The intuitive ways of behaving and responsiveness of virtual marine life further extend profound associations. Whether it's a computerized fish answering client collaborations or the exact developments of a virtual dolphin, the feeling of office and commitment upgrades the client's personal venture. The powerful idea of communications cultivates a view of the virtual marine life as responsive creatures, making a more significant association.

Personalization and Customization

The capacity to customize and modify virtual marine life adds a layer of close to home venture for clients. Whether picking interesting variety designs for virtual fish, making customized aquariums, or choosing individual attributes and ways of behaving, the course of customization permits clients to shape their computerized marine associates. This individual touch cultivates a feeling of pride and connection, developing the profound bond.

IV. Profound Reverberation in Advanced Accounts

Convincing Storylines and Accounts

Computerized stories assume a critical part in summoning profound reactions from clients. Whether a storyline investigates the difficulties looked by virtual marine characters or an undertaking that unfurls in the limitlessness of a computerized sea, convincing stories give setting to close to home commitment.

Clients become put resources into the virtual lives, battles, and wins of marine characters, raising the profound reverberation of the experience.

Protection and Ecological Topics

Integrating protection and ecological topics into computerized stories adds a layer of genuine pertinence, enhancing the profound effect. Clients might wind up exploring difficulties like coral dying, contamination, or overfishing inside the virtual biological system. These stories bring issues to light about ecological issues as well as impart a feeling of obligation and compassion toward the situation of marine life.

V. Mental Parts of Profound Associations

Compassion and Recognizable proof

The foundation of profound associations with virtual marine life frequently includes compassion and distinguishing proof. Clients project their feelings onto advanced marine characters, relating to their battles and encounters. The capacity to sympathize with virtual marine life mirrors the limit of people to broaden their close to home reactions past the limits of this present reality.

Stress Decrease and Prosperity

Research recommends that collaborating with virtual marine life can emphatically affect pressure decrease and generally speaking prosperity. The quieting presence of virtual seas, the relieving developments of fish, and the vivid idea of computerized marine conditions add to a feeling of unwinding and serenity. These positive profound encounters can improve mental prosperity and give a getaway from the burdens of day to day existence.

VI. Instructive and Remedial Applications

Gamified Opportunities for growth

The profound associations shaped with virtual marine life reach out to instructive settings through gamified opportunities for growth. Instructive games influence the allure of marine characters to grant information about sea life science, biological systems, and protection. The close to home commitment upgrades the maintenance of data, transforming learning into a genuinely full and pleasant experience.

Restorative Mediations

Virtual marine life has tracked down applications in remedial mediations, especially for people confronting pressure, nervousness, or certain mental circumstances. Computer generated reality conditions highlighting marine scenes have been utilized as instruments for unwinding and openness treatment.

The close to home associations framed in these virtual conditions add to the restorative advantages, advancing a feeling of quiet and prosperity.

VII. Moral Contemplations and Difficulties

Possible Effect on True Mentalities

While close to home associations with virtual marine life offer positive encounters, there are moral contemplations in regards to their possible effect on true mentalities and ways of behaving. Clients who foster compelling profound bonds with computerized marine characters might move these opinions to their genuine partners. This raises worries about the potential for misconception the intricacies of real marine biological systems and preservation issues.

Adjusting Diversion and Protection

Computerized encounters including virtual marine life frequently endeavor to offset diversion with protection informing. The test lies in guaranteeing that the profound associations framed don't eclipse the instructive and preservation angles. Finding some kind of harmony is vital to encouraging ecological mindfulness without compromising the essential objective of giving a charming client experience.

VIII. Future Patterns and Conceivable outcomes

Progressions in Virtual and Expanded Reality

What's to come holds energizing opportunities for headways in virtual and expanded reality advances. Augmented reality encounters could give clients much more vivid and sensible associations with virtual marine life, further upgrading close to home associations. Increased reality applications could carry marine characters into this present reality, mixing virtual and actual conditions for one of a kind narrating encounters.

Intelligent Resident Science Drives

The mix of virtual marine life into intuitive resident science drives presents a promising pattern. Advanced stages could team up with sea life researchers to gather information on client cooperations, inclinations, and virtual preservation decisions. This information could contribute important experiences into client discernments and ways of behaving connected with marine preservation, possibly helping true logical endeavors.

Chapter 5

Gaming Technologies And Clownfish Realism

Gaming innovations have gone through an exceptional development, changing virtual conditions into multifaceted and vivid universes. Among the different occupants of these advanced domains, clownfish stand apart as famous characters that have developed from early pixels to similar portrayals. This investigation dives into the crossing point of gaming innovations and clownfish authenticity, following the excursion from the unassuming starting points of 2D pixels to the vivid encounters presented by trend setting innovations like augmented experience (VR) and computerized reasoning (simulated intelligence).

II. Pixelated Trailblazers: Clownfish in Early Gaming

Beginning of 2D Pixels

The excursion of clownfish in gaming starts with the beginning of 2D pixels. Restricted by graphical requirements, game engineers presented clownfish as characters exploring oversimplified submerged scenes. The utilization of pixels, while crude by the present principles, established the groundwork for the unmistakable hue and conspicuous examples of clownfish in virtual seas. Regardless of the mechanical impediments, these pixelated pioneers started the creative mind of players and made way for progressions in gaming authenticity.

Imagery in Restricted Detail

The imagery of clownfish was saved even inside the impediments of pixelated illustrations. Designers decisively utilized variety and shape to address clownfish, depending on the notorious orange and white tints to convey their character. While the subtleties were insignificant, the imagery related with clownfish as energetic and fun loving characters persevered, making an early close to home association among players and these advanced marine friends.

III. Headways in Designs: The Jump to 3D Authenticity

Development of Reasonable Portrayals

As gaming innovation advanced, the progress from 2D to 3D illustrations denoted an extraordinary stage for clownfish authenticity. High-goal surfaces, definite displaying, and high level concealing methods permitted designers to make practical portrayals of clownfish. The development of designs innovation assumed a critical part in drawing out the complex subtleties of clownfish life systems, from the surface of their scales to the smooth developments of their blades.

Meticulousness and Conduct

Progressions in illustrations innovation welcomed an elevated concentrate to detail and conduct. Clownfish in 3D domains were as of now not static elements; they showed dynamic developments, sensible swimming examples, and ways of behaving that reflected their genuine partners. The objective was to make a consistent mix of clownfish into virtual seas, upgrading the general gaming experience by catching the embodiment of these marine characters.

IV. Particular Attributes and Capacities of Virtual Clownfish

Little Size, Large Effect

In the domain of gaming, clownfish arose as characters with unmistakable characteristics and capacities that put them aside. Their little size turned into a benefit, permitting players to explore mind boggling submerged conditions effortlessly. The deftness of virtual clownfish, combined with their perky swimming style, acquainted a powerful component with interactivity. Whether dashing through coral reefs or investigating stowed away caverns, the reduced size of virtual clownfish opened up remarkable opportunities for drawing in undertakings.

Cover and Endurance Strategies

Integrating certifiable qualities into ongoing interaction, virtual clownfish frequently had remarkable capacities like cover. Players wound up exploring virtual seas where clownfish could conceal inside coral developments or mix consistently with their environmental factors. These endurance strategies became fundamental to interactivity, introducing moves and vital open doors for players to investigate and dominate.

V. Innovative Progressions: Augmented Reality (VR) and Man-made reasoning (artificial intelligence)

Vivid Encounters with Augmented Reality

The coming of augmented reality (VR) innovation raised clownfish authenticity to extraordinary degrees of drenching. VR headsets permitted players to jump into virtual seas, encountering the submerged world in three-layered space.

The tangible wealth of VR, combined with the capacity to cooperate with the virtual climate in a more natural manner, improved the close to home association among players and their virtual clownfish partners.

Simulated intelligence Driven Ways of behaving for Authenticity

Computerized reasoning (artificial intelligence) assumed an essential part in improving the authenticity of clownfish ways of behaving inside virtual seas. Simulated intelligence driven calculations administered how virtual clownfish answered player activities, ecological changes, and the general movement of the game. The unique idea of simulated intelligence driven ways of behaving guaranteed that virtual clownfish adjusted to various circumstances, making a more vivid and responsive virtual experience.

VI. Instructive Importance: Learning Through Virtual Clownfish

Gamified Opportunities for growth

Past diversion, virtual clownfish became channels for gamified growth opportunities. Players drew in with instructive components consistently woven into interactivity, giving data about clownfish science, ways of behaving, and their job in marine biological systems. These gamified growth opportunities transformed virtual undertakings into amazing open doors for players to secure information about marine life in an intuitive and charming way.

Preservation Informing Through Ongoing interaction

The consideration of virtual clownfish in gaming stories opened roads for consolidating protection informing. Games with ecological subjects brought issues to light about true dangers to marine conditions, like coral dying or overfishing. The presence of preservation components in the storyline, combined with the vivid idea of ongoing interaction, enhanced the effect of protection informing and energized a feeling of natural obligation among players.

VII. Challenges and Moral Contemplations

Adjusting Authenticity and Diversion

Game engineers confronted the continuous test of offsetting authenticity with amusement while depicting virtual clownfish. While authenticity upgraded the vivid nature of gaming encounters, it must be painstakingly adjusted to try not to overpower players with an excess of detail. Finding some kind of harmony guaranteed that the instructive and protection parts of virtual clownfish portrayal didn't eclipse the essential objective of giving a drawing in and agreeable gaming experience.

Moral Contemplations in Virtual Aquariums

The incorporation of virtual aquariums inside gaming conditions raised moral contemplations with respect to the expected commodification of virtual marine species. Players been able to gather and exchange virtual clownfish, reflecting worries about the effect of this present reality aquarium exchange on wild populaces. Game engineers explored the moral ramifications of virtual aquariums to forestall accidental unfortunate results on player insights and true preservation perspectives.

VIII. Future Patterns and Potential outcomes

Progressions in Expanded Reality (AR)

What was in store held energizing prospects with progressions in expanded reality (AR). AR overlays computerized components onto this present reality climate, offering a remarkable mix of virtual and actual encounters. Players might actually associate with virtual clownfish characters in true settings, bringing the sorcery of virtual seas into the day to day existences of players.

Intelligent Resident Science Drives

The incorporation of virtual clownfish into intuitive resident science drives opened opportunities for cooperation between gaming stages and sea life researchers. Information on player associations, inclinations, and virtual preservation decisions could contribute important bits of knowledge into player insights and ways of behaving connected with marine protection, possibly helping true logical endeavors.

5.1 Advancements in Graphics and Animation

In the unique domain of computerized diversion, the development of illustrations and activity has been out and out progressive. From the beginning of pixelated effortlessness to the vivid, exact visuals of today, progressions in innovation have impelled illustrations and activity to remarkable levels. This investigation dives into the astounding excursion of these mechanical wonders, following the development, key achievements, and the significant effect on different enterprises, from gaming to film and then some.

II. Advancement of Illustrations: From Pixels to Photorealism

1. The Pixelated Starting points

   The advancement of illustrations follows its underlying foundations to the pixelated starting points of computerized shows. Early PCs and gaming consoles were restricted by low goals and variety ranges, bringing forth pixel craftsmanship. Games like "Pong" and "Space Trespassers" exhibited basic, blocky illustrations that established the groundwork for the intuitive visual encounters to come. These modest pixels, however essential, started the minds of designers and players the same.

2. Ascent of 2D Designs

   The progress from pixel workmanship to 2D designs denoted a critical jump forward. Games like "Super Mario Brothers." on the

Nintendo Theater setup (NES) exhibited the capability of lively, side-looking over conditions. The characters and scenes turned out to be more definite, offering an all the more outwardly captivating experience. As innovation progressed, the graphical abilities of gaming stages extended, preparing for progressively modern 2D visuals.

3. Rise of 3D Illustrations

The coming of 3D illustrations denoted a change in outlook in the gaming and media outlet. Games like "Super Mario 64" and "Shudder" acquainted players with vivid three-layered universes. This progress took into account more sensible person models, dynamic conditions, and improved profundity insight. The period of 3D designs opened additional opportunities for narrating and interactivity, pushing the limits of what was outwardly attainable.

4. Photorealism and Superior quality Designs

Headways in equipment capacities and delivering advancements delivered a period of photorealistic designs. Games like "The Remainder of Us" and "Unfamiliar 4" exhibited the capacity to establish characters and conditions that moved toward true to life quality. Superior quality illustrations turned into the new norm, offering a remarkable degree of detail and visual devotion. The quest for photorealism turned into a main impetus, obscuring the lines among virtual and reality.

III. Liveliness Upheaval: From Hand-Attracted to CGI

1. Hand-Drawn Activity and the Brilliant Period of Kid's shows

The beginning of activity were described by hand-drawn strategies, with notorious characters like Mickey Mouse and Bugs Rabbit gracing the screens. During the Brilliant Time of Kid's shows, studios like Disney spearheaded the specialty of activity, joining mind boggling hand-attracted casings to make liquid, spellbinding movement. The craftsmanship and innovativeness of illustrators laid the foundation for the narrating force of activity.

2. Presentation of Stop Movement and Claymation

As innovation advanced, artists investigated new methods past hand-drawn liveliness. Stop movement and claymation presented a material and unconventional component to liveliness. Spearheading works like "Ruler Kong" and the manifestations of Beam Harryhausen exhibited the capability of rejuvenating lifeless things outline by outline. These strategies considered remarkable visual styles and added to the expansion of liveliness.

3. Ascent of PC Produced Symbolism (CGI)

The appearance of PC created symbolism (CGI) in the late twentieth century reformed activity. Pixar's "Toy Story," the main full length CGI film, denoted an achievement in liveliness history. CGI gave a degree of authenticity and adaptability beforehand unreachable with conventional techniques. Characters and conditions could now be made and controlled carefully, offering additional opportunities for narrating and visual display.

4. Movement Catch and Execution Liveliness

The reconciliation of movement catch innovation further raised the authenticity of character activity. Entertainers' developments could be made an interpretation of straightforwardly into advanced characters, adding an additional layer of legitimacy to their exhibitions. Films like "Symbol" exhibited the consistent mixing of CGI with movement catch, making characters that felt alive and expressive. Execution liveliness turned into a useful asset for narrators to convey nuanced feelings.

IV. Key Innovative Achievements

1. Designs Handling Units (GPUs)

The presentation of committed Designs Handling Units (GPUs) was a distinct advantage in the realm of illustrations. GPUs, intended to speed up delivering and handling undertakings connected with illustrations, altogether worked on the speed and proficiency of graphical calculations. This headway considered more perplexing and reasonable visuals in both gaming and film, establishing the groundwork for future developments.

2. Beam Following and Continuous Delivering

Beam following, a delivering strategy reenacting the manner in which light connects with virtual items, achieved a jump in visual devotion. Customarily utilized in disconnected delivering, the combination of continuous beam following in gaming motors considered realistic quality designs in intelligent encounters. Games like "Minecraft" and "Control" displayed the shocking lighting and reflections made conceivable by ongoing beam following.

3. High Powerful Reach (HDR) and Wide Variety Range (WCG)

HDR and WCG advancements upgraded the visual experience by growing the scope of varieties and difference. This brought about additional energetic and exact pictures, with a more extensive range of varieties and expanded unique reach. HDR turned into a standard element in shows, offering clients a more vivid and outwardly dazzling involvement with both gaming and film.

4. Brain Organizations and Profound Learning in Activity

The joining of brain organizations and profound learning procedures significantly affects movement. Simulated intelligence driven calculations can now aid undertakings like person movement, looks, and in any event, producing practical scenes. This utilization of simulated intelligence in movement smoothes out the inventive approach, permitting specialists to zero in on more elevated level parts of narrating while at the same time utilizing simulated intelligence for dreary or computational-concentrated undertakings.

V. Junction of Designs and Movement in Gaming

1. Artistic Encounters in Computer games
The intermingling of superior quality illustrations and realistic narrating has changed computer games into vivid true to life encounters. Games like "The Witcher 3: Wild Chase" and "Red Dead Reclamation 2" obscure the lines between customary film and intelligent gaming, conveying accounts with close to home profundity and visual loftiness. Practical person models, itemized conditions, and high level lighting methods add to the making of virtual universes that opponent film creations.

2. Computer generated Reality (VR) and Expanded Reality (AR)

The joining of virtual and expanded reality advances has opened up new boondocks in gaming illustrations and activity. Augmented reality submerges players in completely acknowledged three-layered spaces, offering an unrivaled degree of presence. Games like "Half-Life: Alyx" exhibit the potential for practical conditions and connections. Increased reality, then again, overlays advanced components onto this present reality, making intuitive and outwardly powerful encounters.

VI. Influence on Film and TV

1. Enhanced visualizations in Film
Headways in designs and activity have reclassified the scene of special visualizations in film. CGI has turned into an indispensable piece of filmmaking, considering the formation of fantastical animals, amazing scenes, and stunning successions. Blockbuster films like "Vindicators: Final plan" influence state of the art innovation to

flawlessly mix surprisingly realistic film with CGI, moving crowds to domains beforehand unfathomable.

2. **Real time features and Liveliness Studios**

The ascent of real time features has powered interest for great enlivened content. Activity studios, outfitted with strong delivering advances, produce outwardly dazzling and different substance for worldwide crowds. Unique series and movies from studios like Pixar, Studio Ghibli, and DreamWorks Activity grandstand the imaginative capability of liveliness in conveying convincing accounts with amazing visuals.

VII. Challenges and Moral Contemplations

1. **Uncanny Valley and Authenticity Difficulties**
   As illustrations and liveliness approach photorealism, they experience the peculiarity known as the "uncanny valley." This alludes to the distress or disquiet experienced when a human-like person looks nearly, yet not exactly, sensible. Finding some kind of harmony among authenticity and stylization turns into a sensitive test for makers, guaranteeing that characters and conditions are outwardly engaging without setting off a disrupting reaction.
2. **Moral Contemplations in Deepfakes**

The utilization of profound learning in designs and liveliness presents moral contemplations, especially with regards to deepfakes. Deepfake innovation can control and produce profoundly sensible pictures and recordings, raising worries about deception, wholesale fraud, and the potential for malignant use. The moral ramifications of deepfakes highlight the requirement for dependable turn of events and use of man-made intelligence driven illustrations and activity advances.

VIII. Future Patterns and Conceivable outcomes

1. **Ongoing Cinematography in Games**
   Progressions progressively delivering advances are molding the fate of cinematography in computer games. Games are progressively embracing virtual creation methods, permitting designers to make artistic arrangements continuously. This development obscures the lines between pre-delivered cutscenes and ongoing interaction, offering players a consistent and true to life experience.
2. **Computer based intelligence Created Content and Procedural Movement**

The incorporation of computer based intelligence produced content and procedural liveliness holds guarantee for the eventual fate of designs and movement. Computer based intelligence calculations can help with producing immense and itemized virtual universes, decreasing the weight on specialists and fashioners. Procedural liveliness considers dynamic and responsive person developments, making more vivid and reasonable encounters.

5.2 Realism in Depicting Clownfish Behavior

In the far reaching universe of advanced portrayals, the journey for authenticity stretches out past similar visuals to the nuanced depiction of conduct. Clownfish, with their unmistakable attributes and intriguing ways of behaving, act as convincing subjects for advanced portrayal.

This investigation dives into the complexities of catching the legitimate way of behaving of clownfish in virtual domains, from their social elements to biological collaborations, and the mechanical progressions forming this quest for advanced credibility.

II. The Quintessence of Clownfish Conduct

1. Social Construction and Anemone Holding

   Clownfish, known for their advantageous connection with ocean anemones, show multifaceted social designs. In the wild, they structure family bunches with a predominant reproducing pair and subordinate people. Virtual portrayals of clownfish conduct frequently endeavor to catch the elements of these social designs, depicting the cooperations between people inside a gathering. The holding system with anemones, where clownfish track down shelter and insurance, adds one more layer of intricacy to their virtual way of behaving.

2. Regional Guard and Hostility

   Clownfish are regional animals, vivaciously guarding their anemone homes from likely dangers. In computerized portrayals, this regional way of behaving is passed on through cooperations with other virtual marine life or reproduced gatecrashers. The depiction of animosity, whether as defensive presentations or conflicts with apparent dangers, adds genuineness to the virtual way of behaving of clownfish characters.

3. One of a kind Swimming Examples and Lively Developments

The swimming examples of clownfish, portrayed by dashing developments and energetic jokes, add to their unmistakable appeal. Advanced specialists and illustrators mean to reproduce these novel swimming examples in virtual conditions. The test lies in catching the ease and elegance of clownfish developments, from their quick runs between anemones to the perky whirls that characterize their submerged presence.

III. Mechanical Headways in Conduct Authenticity

1. Activity Apparatus and Skeletal Frameworks
   The groundwork of practical conduct in advanced portrayals lies in complex movement fixing and skeletal frameworks. These frameworks permit illustrators to characterize the skeletal design of virtual characters, deciding how they move and cooperate with their current circumstance. For clownfish, the complexities of balance developments, non-verbal communication, and looks are carefully created utilizing progressed fixing methods to accomplish an elevated degree of conduct legitimacy.

2. Man-made reasoning (computer based intelligence) for Versatile Way of behaving
   The reconciliation of man-made reasoning (computer based intelligence) acquaints a unique component with the way of behaving of virtual clownfish. Artificial intelligence calculations empower virtual characters to adjust their conduct in view of ecological upgrades, client connections, and recreated situations. This versatile conduct reflects the responsiveness of genuine clownfish to changes in their environmental factors, making a more vivid and true computerized insight.

3. Biomechanics Reenactment for Regular Developments

Biomechanics reproduction assumes a significant part in accomplishing normal developments in virtual portrayals of clownfish conduct. By reproducing the material science of submerged development, including water opposition, lightness, and liquid elements, artists can imitate the true swimming examples and movements of clownfish. This thoughtfulness regarding biomechanics adds a layer of authenticity that improves the general trustworthiness of virtual clownfish conduct.

IV. Challenges in Reasonable Conduct Portrayal

1. Offsetting Authenticity with Client Experience
   One of the essential difficulties in portraying reasonable clownfish conduct in computerized conditions is finding some kind of harmony among validness and client experience. While authenticity is pursued for its vivid characteristics, it should not think twice about happiness and commitment of clients. Finding the right balance guarantees that the conduct feels bona fide without turning out to

be excessively intricate or unwieldy for players communicating with virtual clownfish characters.

2. Uncanny Valley and Profound Association

The idea of the uncanny valley, where a computerized character's authenticity arrives at a point that is disrupting for watchers, represents a test in conduct portrayals. Accomplishing a harmony between practical way of behaving and staying away from the uncanny valley is significant to cultivating close to home associations among clients and virtual clownfish. Close to home commitment depends on clients feeling a feeling of commonality and fondness with the computerized characters, and excessively sensible yet somewhat disconcerting way of behaving can obstruct this association.

V. Instructive Meaning of Practical Conduct Portrayal

1. Gamified Learning Conditions
Practical conduct portrayal in virtual clownfish isn't only for diversion; it likewise holds instructive importance. Gamified learning conditions influence the realness of clownfish conduct to bestow information about sea life science, biology, and the significance of coral reef biological systems. Clients can draw in with instructive substance flawlessly woven into ongoing interaction, acquiring bits of knowledge into the way of behaving and natural jobs of clownfish.

2. Preservation Informing through Virtual Encounters

Virtual portrayals of clownfish conduct give a stage to passing on preservation messages. Games and recreations that truly depict the difficulties looked by clownfish right at home, like coral blanching or ecological dangers, add to bringing issues to light about genuine preservation issues. The profound association produced through reasonable conduct improves the effect of protection informing, encouraging a feeling of obligation and ecological stewardship.

VI. Future Patterns in Sensible Conduct Recreation

1. Progressions in AI for Conduct Expectation
What's to come holds energizing prospects with headways in AI for conduct expectation. Via preparing simulated intelligence models on broad datasets of genuine clownfish conduct, designers can make virtual characters equipped for anticipating and adjusting their activities because of different improvements. This prescient conduct

adds a layer of complexity to virtual clownfish communications, making them more unique and responsive.

2. Multiplayer Biological system Reenactments

The reconciliation of multiplayer biological systems in virtual conditions acquaints a cooperative aspect with practical conduct reproduction. Clients can cooperate with one another as well likewise with computer based intelligence driven clownfish characters, adding to the general elements of a computerized marine environment. These multiplayer recreations offer open doors for cooperative learning, examination, and protection endeavors inside virtual environments.

VII. Moral Contemplations in Sensible Conduct Portrayal

1. Obligation in Instructive Substance

Engineers and content makers bear the obligation of guaranteeing that reasonable conduct portrayals, particularly in instructive substance, line up with logical exactness. Deceptions of clownfish conduct or environmental elements can prompt misinterpretations among clients.

Moral contemplations include teaming up with marine specialists to confirm the precision of social data and advancing a nuanced comprehension of marine life.

2. Natural Effect Mindfulness

Sensible conduct portrayals in virtual conditions can likewise act as a stage for advancing natural effect mindfulness. Games and recreations can consolidate stories that feature the results of human exercises on marine biological systems, empowering clients to think about this present reality ramifications of their activities. Moral contemplations include passing on a message of natural obligation without sensationalizing or distorting complex issues.

5.3 Player Engagement and Immersion

In the consistently advancing scene of computerized amusement, player commitment and drenching stand as twin support points that characterize the achievement and effect of intuitive encounters. As innovation progresses, game engineers persistently investigate inventive ways of enamoring players and transport them into vivid universes. This investigation dives into the complex elements of player commitment and inundation, unwinding the mental, mechanical, and plan components that add to the wizardry of convincing computerized encounters.

II. The Pith of Player Commitment

1. Intelligent Accounts and Player Office
   At the core of player commitment lies the idea of intelligent accounts, where players become dynamic members in the unfurling story. Games with expanding storylines, significant decisions, and results enable players with office, permitting them to shape the account in light of their choices. The feeling of control and effect on the game world upgrades commitment, cultivating a customized and contributed insight.

2. Profound Reverberation and Character Connection
   Player commitment rises above simple connection; it dives into the domain of close to home reverberation. Games that unbelievably make characters with profundity, interesting battles, and convincing curves inspire close to home reactions from players. Building an association among players and virtual characters encourages a feeling of sympathy, venture, and a readiness to explore the difficulties introduced in the game.

3. Dynamic Ongoing interaction and Ability Movement

Commitment is supported through unique interactivity that difficulties and prizes players. The feeling of movement, whether through stepping up, securing new capacities, or dominating abilities, powers a player's inherent inspiration.

Very much planned movement frameworks give a ceaseless pride, keeping players put resources into the excursion and anxious to investigate the following test.

III. The Craft of Inundation

1. Practical Conditions and Tasteful Allure
   Submersion depends on the making of practical and tastefully engaging conditions. State of the art designs, scrupulousness, and vivid soundscapes transport players into virtual universes that reflect reality or proposition fantastical scenes. The visual and hear-able constancy of game conditions assumes a crucial part in suspending doubt and bringing players into the vivid embroidery of the gaming experience.

2. Consistent Ongoing interaction and World Attachment
   Consistent ongoing interaction contributes altogether to inundation by disposing of interruptions that could help players to remember the phony of the gaming experience. Smooth changes between scenes, sensible physical science, and a firm world plan make a vivid stream. At the point when players are not continually helped

to remember the basic mechanics or constraints, they are bound to turn out to be completely caught up in the virtual climate.

3. Player Presence in Augmented Simulation (VR)

The coming of computer generated reality (VR) has introduced another time of inundation by setting players straightforwardly inside the advanced domains. VR innovations, including headsets and movement regulators, empower an increased feeling of presence. Players can actually communicate with the virtual climate, whether it's going after objects, investigating spaces, or participating in reasonable developments. The unmistakable sensation of being available in the game world enhances the feeling of submersion.

IV. Mental Components of Commitment and Inundation

1. Stream State and Mental Retention
   Player commitment frequently prompts a mental state known as "stream," an idea presented by therapist Mihaly Csikszentmihalyi. Stream happens when people are completely submerged in a movement, encountering profound fixation and a feeling of immortality. Games that give a fair degree of challenge, coordinated with the player's expertise, can incite a stream state, cultivating supported commitment and pleasure.
2. Presence and Transportation in Vivid Conditions

Submersion depends on mental peculiarities like presence and transportation. Presence alludes to the emotional sensation of being in a virtual climate, while transportation includes the psychological shift from the actual environmental elements to the virtual world. These mental components are pivotal for making a feeling of "being there" inside the game, obscuring the limits among the real world and the computerized insight.

V. Mechanical Progressions and Vivid Encounters

1. Increased Reality (AR) and Blended Reality (MR)
   Notwithstanding VR, increased reality (AR) and blended reality (MR) innovations add to vivid encounters. AR overlays advanced components onto this present reality, improving the player's view of their environmental elements. MR, then again, consolidates advanced and actual real factors, permitting virtual and genuine items to associate. These advances grow the opportunities for intelligent and vivid interactivity past customary screen-based encounters.

2. Haptic Input and Tangible Incorporation

Mechanical developments in haptic criticism add to a more vivid gaming experience by connecting with the feeling of touch. High level haptic gadgets give material input, recreating sensations like effects, vibrations, or surfaces. Coordinating haptic criticism upgrades the tactile wealth of ongoing interaction, permitting players to feel the virtual world in a substantial manner.

VI. Plan Methodologies for Improved Commitment and Submersion

1. Player-Driven Plan and Client Experience (UX)
   Player commitment and inundation are profoundly interlaced with client experience (UX) plan. Player-driven plan focuses on the necessities, inclinations, and feelings of the player. UIs that are instinctive, clear, and non-nosy add to a consistent encounter, permitting players to remain completely drew in without pointless mental burden or disturbances.
2. Dynamic Narrating and Pacing

Dynamic narrating, described by non-straight accounts and versatile pacing, upgrades player commitment. Games that change the story stream in view of player decisions or activities make a more customized and vivid experience. Pacing, including all around coordinated snapshots of strain, investigation, and disclosure, guarantees that players stay enraptured all through their excursion.

VII. Difficulties and Future Patterns

1. Adjusting Openness and Authenticity
   One of the continuous difficulties is tracking down the right harmony among openness and authenticity. While reasonable illustrations and complex ongoing interaction mechanics add to drenching, they can likewise present obstructions for certain players. Finding some kind of harmony that obliges a wide crowd without forfeiting profundity or validness stays a test for designers.
2. Moral Contemplations in Vivid Encounters

The potential for profound submersion raises moral contemplations, particularly in situations where players could turn out to be genuinely impacted or dependent. Designers should consider the likely effect of vivid encounters on emotional well-being and prosperity, integrating highlights that advance solid gaming propensities and give instruments to oversee-ing vivid substance.

Chapter 6

Conservation And Education Through Gaming

The crossing point of gaming, preservation, and training makes a strong nexus that rises above diversion to address genuine difficulties. This investigation dives into the sweeping domain where gaming turns into an impetus for ecological protection and schooling. From encouraging attention to effectively including players in preservation endeavors, the cooperative energy among gaming and ecological stewardship can possibly shape a supportable future.

II. The Force of Gaming for Preservation and Training

1. **Gamification as an Instructive Apparatus**
   Gamification, the combination of game components into non-game settings, has arisen as a groundbreaking instrument for schooling. In the domain of protection, gamified encounters offer connecting with and intelligent stages to convey complex natural ideas. By utilizing the characteristic inspiration of play, teachers can give information, impart a feeling of ecological obligation, and rouse activity.

2. **Virtual Nature and Ecological Reproductions**
   Virtual conditions and reproductions give a remarkable road to clients to investigate and figure out natural frameworks. Games that reenact biological systems, biodiversity, and natural elements offer players a vivid opportunity for growth. Virtual environment permits players to notice the fragile equilibrium of biological systems, grasp the effect of human exercises, and investigate preservation methodologies in a gamble free computerized space.

3. **Preservation Narrating through Games**

Narrating is a strong vehicle for passing on messages, and games succeed at making vivid stories. Preservation narrating through games instructs players about ecological issues as well as ingrains sympathy for the regular world. Games with convincing stories can summon close to home reactions, cultivating a profound association among players and the environments they investigate in virtual domains.

III. Instructive Games for Protection Mindfulness

1. Biodiversity Investigation Games
   Biodiversity investigation games take players on virtual excursions to find and find out about assorted environments and the bunch species they harbor. These games frequently incorporate components of investigation, research, and inventoriing, empowering players to comprehend the lavishness of biodiversity and the significance of protecting it. Genuine models, for example, the investigation of rainforests or coral reefs, act as instructive sceneries for these gaming encounters.

2. Natural Riddle Games
   Puzzle games that rotate around natural critical thinking challenge players to ponder protection issues. These games frequently present situations where players should track down answers for natural difficulties, like contamination, living space annihilation, or environmental change. The demonstration of tackling ecological riddles encourages critical thinking abilities and extends' comprehension players might interpret the intricacies associated with protection.

3. Eco-Reenactment and Asset The executives Games

Eco-reproduction games and asset the board reenactments furnish players with the amazing chance to encounter the outcomes of their choices on virtual biological systems. By overseeing assets, settling on preservation situated decisions, and seeing the effect on the climate, players gain experiences into the fragile equilibrium expected for maintainable living. These games offer an involved way to deal with finding out about the interconnectedness of biological frameworks.

IV. Connecting with Players in Preservation Activity

1. Resident Science Games
   Resident science games overcome any issues among gaming and true protection endeavors. These games include players in logical exploration projects by permitting them to contribute information through interactivity. For instance, players might sort pictures of

natural life, distinguish plant species, or add to environment research. Resident science games transform players into dynamic members in continuous protection drives, changing virtual play into substantial commitments to logical information.

2. **Protection Difficulties and Journeys**

Consolidating preservation difficulties and journeys inside games adds a layer of direction to ongoing interaction. Players can embrace virtual missions that reflect true preservation undertakings, like tidying up virtual conditions, safeguarding jeopardized species, or taking part in reforestation endeavors.

Finishing these journeys propels the game story as well as makes an interpretation of into unmistakable commitments to virtual preservation activities or even genuine drives through associations with natural associations.

3. **Computer generated Reality (VR) Undertakings for Protection**

Computer generated reality (VR) gives a vivid stage to preservation encounters. VR endeavors transport players to distant areas, permitting them to observe protection endeavors firsthand. Whether it's a virtual excursion through a safeguarded public park or an intelligent involvement in natural life restoration, VR brings the real factors of protection work nearer to players. This firsthand openness can impart a need to get a move on and a craving to effectively uphold protection causes.

V. **Protection Gaming Examples of overcoming adversity**

1. **"Eco" - Cooperative Eco-Reenactment**

"Eco" is a cooperative eco-reenactment game that moves players to construct civilizations while limiting their effect on the climate. The game presents interconnected frameworks where players should think about the outcomes of their activities on the biological system, environment, and biodiversity. With a common objective of forestalling natural breakdown, players team up to adjust headway and protection, making "Eco" a striking outcome in advancing eco-cognizant ongoing interaction.

2. **"Zoombinis" - Decisive Reasoning in Nature**

"Zoombinis" is an instructive game that spotlights on rationale, decisive reasoning, and natural ideas. Players guide little animals, Zoombinis, through different difficulties and biological systems. The game acquaints players with environmental standards, like variation, biodiversity, and advantageous interaction, while encouraging critical thinking abilities. "Zoombinis" embodies how instructive games can flawlessly incorporate ecological subjects into drawing in ongoing interaction.

3. "Universe of Warcraft: Fight for Azeroth" - In-Game Protection Missions

Greatly multiplayer online pretending games (MMORPGs) like "Universe of Warcraft" have consolidated in-game protection crusades. In the "Fight for Azeroth" extension, players take part in virtual ecological activism by taking part in journeys connected with safeguarding biological systems, protecting natural life, and battling contamination. These in-game missions add to the general story as well as bring issues to light about true ecological issues.

VI. Difficulties and Contemplations

1. Adjusting Diversion and Instruction
One of the essential difficulties in protection and training through gaming is finding some kind of harmony between amusement esteem and instructive substance. Games should be connecting with and agreeable to catch players' consideration, yet they likewise need to convey significant instructive messages. Striking this harmony guarantees that players remain drenched in the gaming experience while engrossing significant protection information.

2. Inclusivity and Availability

Guaranteeing inclusivity and availability is pivotal for the outcome of protection and schooling games. Game engineers should consider different crowds, including age gatherings, social foundations, and people with shifting degrees of gaming experience. Planning games that take care of an expansive range of players improves the scope and effect of preservation instruction drives.

VII. Future Patterns in Protection Gaming

1. Expanded Reality (AR) Protection Applications
The joining of expanded reality (AR) into protection applications holds guarantee for future drives. AR can overlay instructive data on certifiable conditions, furnishing clients with experiences into nearby biological systems, untamed life, and protection endeavors. By consolidating AR innovation with gaming components, engineers can make intelligent and instructive encounters that mix flawlessly with the players' environmental factors.

2. Blockchain and Protection Gaming Prizes

Blockchain innovation can possibly upset how prizes are appropriated in preservation gaming. By consolidating blockchain-based frameworks, players could get novel advanced resources or tokens as remunerations for their in-game protection endeavors. These computerized resources could address true commitments, encouraging a feeling of responsibility and acknowledgment for players effectively participated in natural preservation inside virtual domains.

6.1 Promoting Environmental Awareness

Natural mindfulness fills in as a key part in tending to the heap difficulties confronting our planet. From environmental change and biodiversity misfortune to contamination and asset exhaustion, the requirement for educated and drew in people has never been more basic. This investigation dives into the diverse procedures utilized to advance ecological mindfulness, including schooling, media, and support endeavors.

By understanding the interconnected idea of these methodologies, we can open the potential for far reaching cognizance and aggregate activity toward a maintainable future.

II. The Job of Schooling in Encouraging Ecological Mindfulness

1. **Formal Ecological Instruction**

   Formal school systems assume a critical part in molding the ecological cognizance of people in the future. Coordinating natural training into school educational programs gives understudies a basic comprehension of biological standards, maintainability, and the effect of human exercises on the climate. Themes like environment science, protection, and ecological morals are woven into subjects going from science to social examinations, encouraging an all encompassing point of view on natural issues.

2. **Experiential Learning and Outside Schooling**

   Experiential learning, especially through outside schooling programs, offers an involved way to deal with natural mindfulness. Field trips, nature strolls, and active exercises drench understudies in common habitats, permitting them to notice biological systems, figure out biodiversity, and witness the interconnectedness of every living thing. These encounters develop environmental information as well as support a feeling of appreciation and stewardship for the regular world.

3. **Local area Commitment and Resident Science**

Instructive drives reach out past the homeroom through local area commitment and resident science projects. Including understudies in neighborhood ecological issues, for example, checking water quality, partaking in tree establishing drives, or leading natural life overviews, imparts a feeling of municipal obligation. These involved ventures engage understudies to add to natural protection endeavors, cultivating a deep rooted obligation to manageable practices effectively.

III. The Impact of Media on Natural Mindfulness

1. Narrative Movies and Natural Stories

   Narrative movies devoted to ecological subjects have the ability to enrapture crowds and bring issues to light on a worldwide scale. Creations like "A Badly designed Truth" and "Before the Flood" have revealed insight into environmental change, provoking conversations and rousing watchers to make a move. The convincing narrating and visual effect of narratives make a close to home association with ecological issues, rising above geological and social limits.

2. Ecological Reporting and News Inclusion

   News sources, through ecological reporting and news inclusion, act as channels for scattering data about squeezing natural issues. Inside and out covering points like deforestation, contamination, and preservation endeavors keeps general society educated and locked in. Ecological writers assume a urgent part in insightful detailing, pointing out issues that require aggregate activity and strategy changes.

3. Web-based Entertainment and Online Stages

The approach of web-based entertainment and online stages has changed the scene of natural correspondence. Crusades, hashtags, and viral substance enhance ecological messages, contacting different crowds around the world. Stages like Instagram, Twitter, and YouTube empower people, associations, and activists to share stories, visuals, and invitations to take action, cultivating a feeling of interconnectedness among a virtual local area of natural backers.

IV. Backing Drives for Natural Mindfulness

1. Grassroots Developments and Local area Activism

   Grassroots developments and local area activism act as impetuses for natural mindfulness at the neighborhood level. Local area based associations, ecological clubs, and lobbyist bunches activate people to resolve natural issues straightforwardly influencing their areas. By encouraging a feeling of local area proprietorship and activism, these drives drive change, bring issues to light, and fabricate an establishment for more extensive natural promotion.

2. Corporate Maintainability and Green Drives
   Organizations and enterprises assume a critical part in forming natural cognizance through feasible practices and green drives. Taking on harmless to the ecosystem arrangements, lessening carbon impressions, and executing roundabout economy standards add to corporate supportability. Organizations that focus on natural obligation set industry principles as well as impact purchaser conduct by advancing eco-accommodating items and practices.
3. Worldwide Cooperation and Strategy Backing

Natural mindfulness is progressed on the worldwide stage through global joint effort and strategy support. Associations, for example, the Assembled Countries Climate Program (UNEP) and non-legislative associations (NGOs) work to bring issues to light, advocate for natural approaches, and work with collaboration among countries. Shows and arrangements, for example, the Paris Settlement on environmental change, embody the aggregate work to address worldwide ecological difficulties through political and strategy channels.

V. Creative Ways to deal with Advance Ecological Mindfulness

1. Gamification for Ecological Schooling
   Gamification use the innate allure of games to draw in and teach people about ecological issues. Instructive games and applications integrate ecological subjects, transforming learning into an intelligent and agreeable experience. Gamified stages urge clients to investigate manageability rehearses, grasp biological ideas, and go with ecologically cognizant decisions in a virtual setting, crossing over diversion and training.
2. Computer generated Reality (VR) Encounters for Ecological Inundation
   Computer generated reality (VR) offers an extraordinary road for vivid ecological encounters. VR stages permit clients to investigate virtual biological systems, witness the effect of environmental change, and participate in preservation situations. These vivid encounters bring out an instinctive comprehension of ecological difficulties, cultivating sympathy and a need to keep moving among clients. VR innovations make a scaffold between computerized reenactments and true natural mindfulness.
3. Workmanship and Innovative Articulation for Natural Promotion

Imaginative articulations, including visual expressions, music, and execution, act as incredible assets for natural promotion. Workmanship conveys complex natural messages in a generally open language, getting close to home reactions and provoking reflection. Public craftsmanship establishments, natural photography displays, and eco-themed exhibitions add to forming public insights and cultivating a more profound association with natural issues.

VI. Difficulties and Contemplations in Advancing Natural Mindfulness

1. Conquering Data Over-burden

   During a time of data over-burden, slicing through the commotion to successfully pass on natural messages represents a test. Making clear, succinct, and significant correspondence procedures is fundamental for catch and hold crowd consideration. The utilization of visual narrating, infographics, and effectively absorbable substance distils complex ecological data for assorted crowds.

2. Tending to Natural Exhaustion

Natural exhaustion, described by a feeling of overpower and weakness even with overwhelming ecological difficulties, represents a mental boundary to mindfulness. Offsetting mindfulness crusades with messages of trust, strengthening, and unmistakable arrangements mitigates exhaustion. Underlining individual activities and exhibiting examples of overcoming adversity adds to a more sure and activity situated story.

VII. Future Patterns in Natural Mindfulness Drives

1. Increased Reality (AR) Instructive Apparatuses

   The joining of expanded reality (AR) into instructive devices holds guarantee for intelligent and customized natural learning. AR applications can overlay ecological data on actual environmental elements, making dynamic and drawing in growth opportunities. By mixing advanced satisfied with this present reality, AR upgrades the openness and adequacy of ecological instruction drives.

2. Customized Eco-Measurements and Maintainability Following

Innovative progressions empower the improvement of customized eco-measurements and supportability following instruments. Applications and stages that permit people to follow their ecological impression, put forth maintainability objectives, and get customized criticism advance a culture of responsibility. These instruments engage people to settle on informed decisions, measure their effect, and effectively add to an aggregate obligation to maintainability.

6.2 Partnerships between Gaming Industry and Conservation Efforts

In the steadily growing scene of computerized diversion, the gaming business has arisen as a strong power with unrivaled reach and impact. Simultaneously, worldwide natural difficulties have highlighted the earnest requirement for aggregate activity to protect our planet. This investigation dives into the extraordinary capability of associations between the gaming business and preservation endeavors. By saddling the vivid idea of games, these joint efforts bring issues to light as well as drive true effect in the domain of natural preservation.

II. The Gaming Business' Effect and Impact

1. The Compass of Gaming Stages

Gaming stages have become universal, contacting assorted crowds across age gatherings, societies, and topographies. From portable gaming to reassure and PC gaming, the business' huge environment gives an interesting road to commitment. With a huge number of dynamic players around the world, gaming stages offer an extraordinary chance to spread data, impact conduct, and motivate aggregate activity.

2. Vivid Encounters and Profound Commitment

One of the trademark highlights of the gaming business is its capacity to make vivid encounters that dazzle players on close to home and scholarly levels. Games rise above conventional types of media by permitting players to effectively partake in stories, decide, and experience outcomes. This vivid commitment cultivates close to home associations, making it a powerful device for conveying complex subjects like natural preservation.

3. Adaptation Models and Social Effect

The adaptation models inside the gaming business, remembering for game buys, microtransactions, and memberships, add to income streams that can be bridled for social effect. Gaming organizations have perceived the possibility to adjust benefit intentions to altruistic undertakings, coordinating assets toward preservation projects, maintainability drives, and ecological backing.

III. The Rise of Eco-Gaming and Green Drives

1. Eco-Gaming: Games with a Reason

Eco-gaming addresses a type of games unequivocally planned with natural topics and protection objectives. These games go past amusement, integrating instructive components, certifiable effect, and maintainability standards. Players are engaged as well as effectively add to natural causes through their in-game activities. Eco-gaming makes way for significant associations between the gaming business and preservation associations.

2. Green Drives and Economical Practices

Gaming organizations have progressively embraced green drives and economical practices to limit their ecological impression. From energy-productive server farms to eco-accommodating bundling and decreased fossil fuel byproducts, the business perceives its liability to take on reasonable practices. These drives show a promise to natural stewardship and give an establishment to cooperative endeavors with protection associations.

IV. Cooperative Organizations: Gaming Industry Meets Protection

1. Instructive Partnerships for Ecological Proficiency
Joint efforts between the gaming business and instructive establishments cultivate natural proficiency. Games intended for instructive purposes, lined up with educational plan targets, add to a really captivating and successful opportunity for growth. By integrating natural topics, these instructive unions furnish understudies with information about protection challenges, biological standards, and the significance of maintainable practices.

2. Protection Associations and In-Game Missions
Protection associations influence the broad reach of gaming stages to run in-game missions. These missions bring issues to light about unambiguous ecological issues, energize manageable ways of behaving, and brief players to add to preservation causes. In-game buys, gifts, or cooperation in virtual occasions inside the gaming climate convert into certifiable help for protection drives.

3. Corporate Social Obligation (CSR) Drives

Many gaming organizations have embraced corporate social obligation (CSR) drives that stretch out past monetary commitments. By effectively taking part in preservation projects, sorting out tree-establishing occasions, or supporting untamed life restoration endeavors, gaming organizations adjust their business goals to natural stewardship. These drives grandstand a guarantee to maintainability and add to the more extensive story of corporate obligation.

V. Examples of overcoming adversity: Gaming and Preservation Effect

1. **"Ocean of Criminals" and Sea Protection**
   The game "Ocean of Criminals" consistently incorporates components of sea investigation, privateer experiences, and natural mindfulness. As a team with the player local area, the game presented a virtual cleanup drive called "The Reviled Sails," where players by and large attempted to tidy up in-game oceans. This drive brought issues to light about sea preservation as well as made an interpretation of in-game endeavors into genuine gifts to marine protection associations.

2. **"Eco" - A Cooperative Eco-Reenactment**
   The game "Eco" is a cooperative eco-reenactment where players team up to fabricate developments while limiting their effect on the climate. This special methodology stresses the interconnectedness of in-game environments and urges players to go with choices that lead to reasonable results. The game encourages a feeling of shared liability, lining up with more extensive preservation objectives and advancing ecological mindfulness.

3. **"Plants versus Zombies: Fight for Neighborville" and Pollinator Preservation**

As a team with the non-benefit Pollinator Organization, the game "Plants versus Zombies: Fight for Neighborville" presented a virtual occasion based on pollinator protection. Players participated in-game exercises, like establishing virtual blossoms, to open rewards and add to genuine drives supporting pollinator-accommodating natural surroundings. This hybrid among gaming and preservation epitomizes the potential for positive effect through imaginative joint efforts.

VI. Difficulties and Contemplations in Gaming-Protection Organizations

1. **Adjusting Amusement and Promotion**
   One of the essential difficulties lies in finding some kind of harmony among amusement and promotion inside gaming encounters. Games should stay pleasant and connecting with for players while actually passing on preservation messages. Finding the balance between story submersion and instructive substance is urgent to guarantee that players eagerly take part in drives without feeling overpowered or separated.

2. **Guaranteeing Credibility and Effect**

Genuineness is vital in gaming-preservation associations to construct entrust with players and partners. Protection drives inside games ought to line up with certifiable effect, and the results ought to be straightforwardly conveyed. Exhibiting unmistakable outcomes, whether through monetary commitments, local area commitment, or biological upgrades, improves the believability of gaming-industry-drove preservation endeavors.

VII. Future Patterns in Gaming-Preservation Coordinated efforts

1. Increased Reality (AR) Protection Encounters

   The mix of expanded reality (AR) into gaming encounters holds enormous potential for protection coordinated efforts. AR can overlay virtual components onto this present reality, making intelligent and instructive preservation encounters. Players could participate in AR missions that include true cleanup exercises, biodiversity observing, or intuitive learning modules that advance natural mindfulness.

2. Blockchain for Straightforward Effect Following

Blockchain innovation presents a chance to improve straightforwardness in following the effect of gaming-protection coordinated efforts. By using blockchain for secure and straightforward record-keeping, partners can follow monetary commitments, measure environmental results, and confirm the credibility of protection drives. This innovation guarantees responsibility and fabricates certainty among players and protection accomplices.

6.3 Educational Value of Virtual Marine Environments

The investigation of virtual marine conditions has arisen as a groundbreaking device in schooling, offering understudies vivid and intelligent encounters that rise above conventional study hall limits. As innovation keeps on progressing, virtual marine conditions give a novel chance to upgrade sea education, natural comprehension, and ecological stewardship. In this investigation, we dive into the instructive worth of virtual marine conditions, looking at how they add to a more profound enthusiasm for marine environments, biodiversity, and the significance of sea protection.

1. Prologue to Virtual Marine Conditions
1. Definition and Extension

   Virtual marine conditions allude to carefully mimicked biological systems that duplicate the submerged world. These conditions can go from sensible, high-constancy recreations to adapted, instructive games. By utilizing advancements like computer generated experience (VR) and expanded reality (AR), understudies can investigate marine life, biological systems, and submerged scenes in a vivid and drawing in way.

2. **Advances Forming Virtual Marine Instruction**

1. **Computer generated Reality (VR):** VR innovation transports clients to completely recreated conditions. In virtual marine training, VR headsets submerge understudies in 360-degree submerged scenes, permitting them to investigate coral reefs, marine life, and submerged geography as though they were jumping.

2. **Expanded Reality (AR):** AR overlays advanced data onto this present reality. With regards to virtual marine conditions, AR can upgrade instructive materials, giving extra data about marine species, environments, and preservation endeavors through cell phones or AR glasses.

3. **Recreations and Instructive Games:** Intuitive reproductions and instructive games offer a gamified way to deal with marine schooling. These encounters frequently consolidate components of diversion with instructive substance, empowering dynamic support and information maintenance.

II. Benefits of Virtual Marine Conditions in Schooling

1. **Availability and Inclusivity**
Virtual marine conditions separate geological hindrances, carrying marine training to landlocked regions or locales without direct admittance to the sea. Understudies overall can profit from these encounters, democratizing marine training and guaranteeing that a different scope of students can investigate and value the marvels of the submerged world.

2. **Experiential Learning and Commitment**
Experiential learning is a foundation of successful schooling, and virtual marine conditions give a powerful stage to vivid encounters. As opposed to depending entirely on course books or recordings, understudies effectively draw in with marine biological systems, noticing marine life, grasping environmental cycles, and investigating submerged natural surroundings. This involved methodology upgrades maintenance and encourages a feeling of interest and miracle.

3. **Wellbeing and Moral Contemplations**
True marine investigation accompanies inborn dangers and moral contemplations. Virtual marine conditions offer a protected and controlled space for picking up, wiping out the likely natural effect of actual visits to sensitive marine biological systems. Furthermore,

moral worries connected with natural life aggravation or living space obliteration are avoided in virtual settings.

4. Interdisciplinary Learning Open doors

Marine instruction frequently includes a multidisciplinary approach, consolidating components of science, biology, ecological science, geology, from there, the sky is the limit. Virtual marine conditions give an all encompassing opportunity for growth, permitting understudies to investigate the interconnected idea of marine environments and grasp the jobs of different disciplines in sea life science and protection.

III. Uses of Virtual Marine Conditions in Schooling

1. Sea life Science and Nature Courses
   Virtual marine conditions are indispensable to sea life science and nature courses at different instructive levels. Understudies can basically take apart marine life forms, notice their way of behaving, and investigate the complexities of marine food networks. These encounters supplement conventional learning strategies and proposition a more powerful comprehension of marine life.

2. Oceanography Studies
   Oceanography, the investigation of the physical and compound properties of the sea, benefits essentially from virtual marine conditions. Understudies can investigate sea flows, temperature varieties, and submerged topographical elements. Reproductions empower them to observe the effect of elements like environmental change on the sea climate.

3. Natural Science and Protection Training
   Understanding the significance of marine preservation is pivotal for encouraging natural stewardship. Virtual marine conditions work with training on issues like coral blanching, overfishing, plastic contamination, and the significance of marine safeguarded regions. Understudies can observer the outcomes of human exercises on marine biological systems and investigate potential protection techniques.

4. Effort and Public Mindfulness Projects

Past conventional training, virtual marine conditions are important instruments for effort and public mindfulness programs. Science focuses, galleries, and natural associations use VR encounters to connect with general society in marine preservation accounts. These drives intend to bring issues to light, move activity, and ingrain a feeling of obligation toward the seas.

IV. Instances of Virtual Marine Schooling Stages

1. TheBlu

   "TheBlu" is a computer generated simulation experience that drenches clients in a striking and practical submerged world. Clients can investigate different sea conditions, experience marine species, and find out about the interconnectedness of marine biological systems. "TheBlu" fills in to act as an illustration of how VR can make an outwardly dazzling and instructive marine experience.

2. Sea Odyssey by Public Geographic

   Public Geographic's "Sea Odyssey" consolidates expanded reality with an actual book to give an intuitive marine opportunity for growth. By filtering pages with a cell phone, clients can open 3D models of marine creatures, access extra data, and take part in intelligent tests. This approach mixes customary instructive materials with state of the art innovation.

3. AquaSim VR

AquaSim VR is a computer generated experience reproduction intended for instructive organizations. It permits clients to investigate a coral reef environment, cooperate with marine life, and find out about coral science. The reenactment consolidates instructive modules on points like coral dying, cooperative connections, and the significance of coral reefs in biodiversity.

V. Difficulties and Contemplations in Virtual Marine Schooling

1. Innovative Hindrances

   Admittance to the important innovation, like VR headsets or AR gadgets, may represent a test for a few instructive foundations. The expense of executing virtual marine schooling programs and guaranteeing fair access for all understudies can be a restricting component.

2. Adjusting Authenticity and Instructive Substance

   While authenticity is significant for a vivid encounter, finding some kind of harmony between enthralling visuals and instructive substance is fundamental. Virtual marine conditions ought to focus on exact portrayals of marine biological systems and species while guaranteeing that instructive targets are met.

3. Advancing Innovation and Educational plan Coordination

The quick development of innovation requires progressing transformation of instructive substance and reconciliation into educational programs. Instructors need admittance to refreshed virtual marine conditions that line up with current logical comprehension and preservation needs.

VI. Future Patterns in Virtual Marine Training

1. Mix with Resident Science Drives
   Virtual marine conditions may progressively incorporate with resident science drives, permitting understudies to add to true research. Understudies could take part in virtual information assortment, screen marine species, and take part in cooperative tasks that add to how we might interpret the seas.
2. Improved Intuitiveness through Man-made reasoning (simulated intelligence)

The mix of man-made intelligence in virtual marine conditions holds guarantee for improved intuitiveness. Computer based intelligence calculations could empower more unique and responsive recreations, permitting marine life inside the virtual climate to show exact ways of behaving and answer client cooperations, making a more legitimate growth opportunity.

Chapter 7

Challenges And Controversies

In the multifaceted embroidered artwork of our globalized society, difficulties and discussions saturate different features of life. These intricacies emerge from financial, social, natural, political, innovative, and wellbeing related factors, making a scene that requests nuanced understanding and capable route. This investigation digs into the diverse elements of difficulties and contentions, revealing their complexities and the basic of tending to them.

Meaning of Difficulties and Contentions

Challenges incorporate deterrents and hardships that hinder progress or make ominous circumstances. They range from monetary inconsistencies and ecological debasement to social polarization and political disturbances. Discussions, then again, include questions, conflicts, and discussions encompassing issues that evoke contradicting perspectives. These may rise up out of social conflicts, moral predicaments, or clashing political belief systems.

Significance of Tending to Difficulties and Contentions

Recognizing and tending to difficulties and contentions are fundamental for cultivating cultural strength and progress. Overlooking or dismissing these issues can prompt far and wide results, affecting economies, social orders, and biological systems. By understanding the underlying drivers and intricacies intrinsic in these difficulties, social orders can figure out informed systems, cultivate discourse, and work toward manageable arrangements.

II. Financial Difficulties

Worldwide Financial Imbalance

Perhaps of the most squeezing challenge in the contemporary world is the unavoidable issue of worldwide monetary imbalance. Abberations in abundance conveyance among countries and inside social orders add to social turmoil and obstruct the accomplishment of supportable advancement objectives. The extending hole between the rich and the poor compounds social strains and represents a danger to the security of economies around the world.

Effect of Innovative Advances on Business

The quick progression of innovation, especially in robotization and computerized reasoning, presents a double edged blade as a test. While mechanical advancement improves effectiveness and development, it simultaneously upsets customary work markets. Mechanization replaces physical work, raising worries about joblessness and the requirement for reskilling the labor force to adjust to the requests of the advanced time.

Monetary Market Unpredictability

Monetary market instability stays an intermittent test, impacted by elements like international occasions, financial slumps, and speculative exercises. Unexpected variances in securities exchanges, money values, and ware costs can significantly affect worldwide economies, influencing organizations, financial backers, and people. Relieving the dangers related with monetary market unpredictability requires cautious oversight and compelling administrative measures.

Exchange Wars and Protectionism

The resurgence of exchange wars and the ascent of protectionist approaches present huge difficulties to worldwide monetary steadiness. Countries taking part in duty questions and raising exchange hindrances disturb laid out supply chains, heighten strains, and hose monetary development. Finding some kind of harmony between public interests and worldwide collaboration is a fragile undertaking, requiring political artfulness to explore the intricacies of the worldwide exchange scene.

III. Social and Social Difficulties

Social Conflicts in a Globalized World

In an interconnected world, social conflicts are unavoidable as different social orders collaborate. Globalization works with the trading of thoughts, values, and customs, yet it additionally emphasizes social contrasts. Exploring these conflicts requires social capability and open exchange to cultivate common comprehension and congruity in a multicultural scene.

Virtual Entertainment and Disinformation

The ascent of virtual entertainment has changed correspondence however has likewise brought about difficulties, outstandingly the spread of disinformation. Control of general assessment, the spread of phony news, and the enhancement of polarizing stories present dangers to cultural attachment. Handling this challenge includes media proficiency instruction, mindful stage administration, and cooperative endeavors to counter disinformation.

Personality Governmental issues and Polarization

Personality legislative issues, energized by the prioritization of gathering characters over shared values, has prompted expanded polarization in social orders. Troublesome way of talking and the propagation of "us against them" attitudes strain social union. Cultivating inclusivity, advancing discourse, and tending to basic cultural divisions are fundamental stages in relieving the effects of personality legislative issues.

Difficulties of Urbanization

Quick urbanization presents difficulties connected with foundation, lodging, and asset the executives. The grouping of populaces in metropolitan regions strains fundamental administrations, prompting issues like gridlock, lacking lodging, and ecological debasement. Practical metropolitan preparation, interests in foundation, and local area commitment are urgent in tending to the difficulties related with the worldwide pattern of urbanization.

IV. Natural Difficulties

Environmental Change and A dangerous atmospheric devation

Environmental change and a dangerous atmospheric devation stand as existential dangers, rising above geological limits and influencing biological systems around the world. The ascent in ozone depleting substance emanations, deforestation, and modern exercises add to climbing temperatures, outrageous climate occasions, and disturbances to environments. Tending to environmental change requires global participation, manageable practices, and a guarantee to decreasing carbon impressions.

Biodiversity Misfortune and Environment Corruption

The deficiency of biodiversity and debasement of environments imperil the fragile equilibrium of the planet's normal frameworks. Human exercises like deforestation, overfishing, and living space obliteration add to the downfall of species and upset biological balance. Protection endeavors, natural surroundings rebuilding, and feasible asset the executives are fundamental in saving biodiversity and keeping up with environment wellbeing.

Contamination and Natural Corruption

The inescapable issue of contamination, incorporating air, water, and soil contamination, presents extreme dangers to ecological and human wellbeing. Modern poisons, plastic waste, and substance toxins corrupt environments and damage biodiversity. Carrying out severe ecological guidelines, advancing feasible practices, and putting resources into clean advancements are essential in tending to the complex difficulties of contamination.

Asset Consumption and Overconsumption

The impractical consumption of normal assets, driven by overconsumption and shifty practices, overburdens the planet's limited assets. Over-extraction of water, exhaustion of fisheries, and extreme utilization of non-sustainable power sources add to asset shortage. Progressing to roundabout economies, advancing mindful utilization, and embracing environmentally friendly power sources are basic for feasible asset the executives.

V. Political Difficulties

Dangers to A majority rule government

Difficulties to vote based standards and foundations have become progressively common, appearing in issues like disintegration of press opportunity, assaults on law and order, and constituent obstruction. Defending majority rules system requires fortifying popularity based organizations, advancing straightforwardness, and encouraging community commitment to maintain the upsides of popularity based administration.

Ascent of Tyranny

The ascent of tyranny presents a critical test to vote based standards and common freedoms. Tyrant systems frequently reduce common freedoms, stifle dispute, and move power in the possession of a couple. Global judgment, support for common society, and political endeavors are critical in tending to the difficulties presented by the ascent of tyranny.

Political Defilement and Embarrassments

Political defilement sabotages the confidence in administration and hampers the successful working of vote based organizations. Pay off, theft, and nepotism dissolve public certainty and block financial turn of events. Battling political defilement requires vigorous enemy of debasement measures, free oversight, and a pledge to responsibility and straightforwardness.

Exile and Movement Emergency

The worldwide exile and movement emergency presents complex difficulties, powered by clashes, oppression, and natural variables. Overseeing mass developments of individuals requires global participation, helpful help, and tending to the main drivers of uprooting. Finding some kind of harmony between public safety concerns and compassionate contemplations is fundamental in exploring the difficulties related with relocation.

VI. Innovative Difficulties

Moral Predicaments in Man-made brainpower

The coming of man-made brainpower (computer based intelligence) presents moral predicaments, including worries about protection, predisposition in calculations, and the possible abuse of artificial intelligence in observation. Creating moral systems, managing simulated intelligence applications, and encouraging public mindfulness are fundamental in exploring the moral difficulties presented by the quick progressions in artificial intelligence.

Network safety Dangers

The interconnected idea of the computerized world opens social orders to online protection dangers, including hacking, information breaks, and digital undercover work. Safeguarding basic foundation, improving online protection measures, and global coordinated effort are fundamental in tending to the difficulties presented by digital dangers.

Security Worries in the Advanced Age

The expansion of computerized advances raises critical protection worries, with individual information turning out to be progressively helpless against observation and double-dealing. Laying out powerful information security guidelines, engaging people with command over their information, and advancing computerized proficiency are significant in defending protection in the advanced age.

Computerized Gap and Mechanical Imbalance

While mechanical headways offer open doors, a computerized partition continues, making variations in admittance to data and open doors. Connecting the computerized partition expects endeavors to give widespread admittance to innovation, upgrade advanced education, and address financial variables that add to mechanical disparity.

VII. Wellbeing Difficulties

Worldwide Wellbeing Pandemics

The development of worldwide wellbeing pandemics, as exemplified by the Coronavirus emergency, features the interconnectedness of wellbeing challenges. Containing irresistible illnesses, guaranteeing worldwide antibody dissemination, and reinforcing general wellbeing framework are critical in tending to the wellbeing challenges presented by pandemics.

7.1 Ethical Concerns in Depicting Marine Life in Games

The portrayal of marine life in computer games has developed into an enamoring and vivid part of virtual encounters, permitting players to investigate the miracles of submerged environments. Notwithstanding, this virtual investigation raises moral worries that stretch out past the gaming screen. This investigation digs into the moral contemplations encompassing the depiction of marine life in games, looking at liabilities of game engineers, the effect on player conduct, and the potential for positive genuine effect.

1. Meaning of Marine Life Portrayals in Games

    The portrayal of marine life in games goes past simple diversion; it shapes discernments, impacts player conduct, and, possibly, adds to genuine protection endeavors. As innovation takes into account progressively reasonable and intelligent virtual seas, the moral ramifications of these portrayals become more articulated.

2. The Crossing point of Amusement and Moral Contemplations

Adjusting the diversion worth of games with moral principles represents a mind boggling challenge. This investigation plans to reveal insight into the moral contemplations game designers should explore, the impact of player activities on virtual marine environments, and the potential for positive certifiable ramifications emerging from dependable game turn of events.

II. Moral Contemplations in Game Turn of events

1. Portrayal Exactness and Generalizing
   Guaranteeing the exact portrayal of marine life is an essential moral thought in game turn of events. Deluding portrayals or propagation of generalizations can add to public mistaken assumptions about marine species. Game designers should focus on precision, attracting from logical information to really depict different marine biological systems.

2. Preservation and Supportability Accounts
   Games have the possibility to be strong backers for marine protection and manageability. Moral game advancement includes consolidating stories that feature the significance of safeguarding marine biological systems, tending to ecological dangers, and advancing manageable practices. By meshing preservation messages into game plots, engineers can add to bringing issues to light and encouraging a feeling of obligation among players.

3. Effect of Game Mechanics on Marine Life
   Game mechanics assume an essential part in forming player communications with virtual marine conditions. Moral worries emerge when game mechanics boost hurtful activities, for example, overfishing or damaging ways of behaving impersonating genuine dangers to marine life. Engineers should cautiously think about the outcomes of in-game activities and guarantee that ongoing interaction lines up with moral standards, empowering positive and capable commitment.

4. Social Awareness and Native Viewpoints

Integrating social responsiveness and regarding native viewpoints on marine life are necessary parts of moral game turn of events. Native people group frequently have profound associations with marine conditions and explicit social convictions in regards to marine species. Game engineers ought to participate in significant counsel with native networks, keeping away from appointment and guaranteeing that portrayals line up with social qualities and natural stewardship.

III. The Impact of Player Conduct

1. Effect of In-Game Activities on Virtual Marine Environments
   Players' activities inside virtual marine conditions can have enduring outcomes on the recreated biological systems. Moral game plan considers the environmental effect of in-game decisions, advancing preservation disapproved of navigation. Players ought to be made mindful that their virtual activities can impact the wellbeing and equilibrium of the virtual marine world, cultivating a feeling of obligation and natural mindfulness.

2. Instructive Worth versus Shifty Ongoing interaction
   Games act as both diversion and instructive devices. Moral game plan use this possibility to give information about marine life, biological systems, and protection challenges. Finding some kind of harmony between instructive worth and amusement is significant to keep away from shady ongoing interaction that focuses on emotionalism over precise portrayal and capable ecological accounts.

3. Support of Ecological Stewardship

Games can add to the development of ecological stewardship by building up sure ways of behaving and esteems. Moral contemplations include integrating prizes or acknowledgment for activities that line up with protection objectives. By building up natural stewardship inside the game world, engineers can urge players to move these qualities to true settings, encouraging a feeling of obligation toward the security of marine environments.

IV. Genuine Ramifications and Preservation Endeavors

1. Making an interpretation of In-Game Encounters to Genuine Effect
   The moral obligation of game designers stretches out past the virtual domain. Games can possibly rouse true activity and backing for marine protection. Moral game improvement includes making pathways for players to make an interpretation of their virtual encounters into substantial commitments to marine preservation endeavors. This could incorporate associations with protection associations, virtual

occasions that trigger genuine activities, or in-game buys that store certifiable drives.

2. **Joint effort with Preservation Associations**
Moral game improvement includes fashioning associations with protection associations to guarantee that virtual portrayals line up with logical information and preservation objectives. Cooperative endeavors can give designers significant experiences, advance exact portrayal, and influence the gaming local area's excitement to help preservation drives. Such coordinated efforts add to a positive effect on marine biological systems both practically and truly.

3. **Player Commitment in Certifiable Preservation Drives**

Moral contemplations reach out to enabling players to participate in true preservation drives effectively. Games can act as stages for gathering pledges, mindfulness missions, or resident science projects. Moral game plan includes coordinating highlights that work with direct commitments, for example, in-game buys with continues coordinated to preservation projects or virtual occasions that harmonize with genuine protection endeavors.

V. Contextual analyses: Looking at Moral Methodologies in Game Plan

1. **Positive Instances of Moral Marine Life Portrayals**
A few games embody moral ways to deal with marine life portrayals, consolidating diversion with dependable stories. "Past Blue," for example, gives a connecting with submerged investigation experience while incorporating instructive substance about sea life science and preservation. The game cultivates an appreciation for marine life while accentuating the significance of ecological assurance.

2. **Examples of Moral Omissions and Contentions**

In any case, not all games effectively explore the moral intricacies related with marine life portrayals. Cases of moral breaches and contentions feature the difficulties designers face in offsetting amusement with capable depictions. Analyzing these cases gives significant illustrations to the business, encouraging consistent improvement in moral game turn of events.

VI. Moral Systems for Game Engineers

1. **Rules for Moral Marine Life Portrayals**
Creating and sticking to moral structures is fundamental for game

designers. Clear rules for moral marine life portrayals can incorporate precision norms, evasion of generalizations, and standards of social awareness. Laying out a bunch of moral rules assists designers with exploring the intricacies of virtual marine conditions capably.

2. **Cooperative Methodologies with Protection Specialists**
Teaming up with sea life researcher, environmentalists, and protection specialists is a proactive move toward guaranteeing moral game turn of events. Integrating logical aptitude assists engineers with making precise portrayals of marine life and biological systems. Moreover, cooperation gives bits of knowledge into protection stories, encouraging a more grounded association between virtual encounters and genuine preservation endeavors.

3. **Consolidating Moral Contemplations in Game Evaluations**

Game rating frameworks assume an essential part in directing purchasers and guardians. Coordinating moral contemplations into game appraisals, for example, assessing portrayals of marine life, can advise players about the moral obligation regarding designers. Straightforward correspondence through game appraisals helps shape player assumptions and urges the business to focus on moral contemplations.

VII. Future Patterns and Mechanical Arrangements

1. **Headways in artificial intelligence and Conduct Biology**
Headways in man-made brainpower (man-made intelligence) and social environment present energizing open doors for improving the moral elements of marine life portrayals. Man-made intelligence calculations can mimic sensible ways of behaving of virtual marine species, adding to additional credible and mindful depictions. Coordinating social environment standards guarantees that in-game connections line up with the normal ways of behaving of marine life.

2. **Increased Reality (AR) and Certifiable Connections**
Expanded reality (AR) opens additional opportunities for associating virtual encounters with this present reality. Moral game improvement can use AR to urge players to investigate and find out about marine life in their genuine environmental elements. This innovation overcomes any barrier between the virtual and genuine, cultivating a more profound comprehension of the significance of marine protection.

3. **Blockchain Innovation for Straightforward Effect Following**

Blockchain innovation offers a straightforward and secure method for following the effect of virtual encounters on certifiable preservation endeavors. By executing blockchain in games, engineers can give obvious proof of commitments to protection projects, guaranteeing that in-game buys or activities bring about unmistakable advantages for marine biological systems.

7.2Impact of Gaming on Real-World Conservation

The unique convergence of gaming and protection has developed into a strong power for positive change in reality. Gaming, when basically seen as a wellspring of diversion, has risen above its conventional limits to turn into an impetus for ecological mindfulness, schooling, and activity. This investigation dives into the extraordinary capability of gaming, inspecting what virtual encounters can convert into unmistakable means for on worldwide preservation endeavors.

1. The Crossing point of Gaming and Preservation

    The intermingling of gaming and preservation addresses a noteworthy collaboration, where the vivid idea of virtual encounters is outfit to address genuine ecological difficulties. What was once a domain of diversion has developed into a stage equipped for impacting mentalities, ways of behaving, and cultivating a feeling of obligation towards the planet.

2. The Capability of Games to Drive Genuine Effect

As innovation propels, gaming arises as a medium with the possibility to contribute essentially to protection drives. Game designers, frequently teaming up with natural associations, influence the enthralling appeal of virtual universes to motivate players to draw in with and effectively add to certifiable protection endeavors. The effect of gaming on preservation stretches out past diversion, offering a remarkable road for worldwide ecological stewardship.

II. The Force of Natural Stories in Games

1. Creating Convincing Preservation Stories

    At the core of the effect of gaming on true preservation lies the capacity of games to recount convincing and sincerely resounding stories. Protection themed games utilize many-sided stories that submerge players in the difficulties looked by the regular world. Whether exploring through imperiled biological systems, battling environmental change, or safeguarding untamed life, these stories act as amazing assets to bring out compassion and make a profound association among players and the genuine protection issues they address.

2. Impact on Player Viewpoints and Values

The groundbreaking force of gaming becomes obvious as players are presented to accounts that go past simple diversion. Protection themed games assume a urgent part in molding player points of view and values. By giving an intelligent stage to encounter ecological difficulties first-hand, games encourage an uplifted consciousness of the significance of preservation. The close to home effect of these virtual encounters frequently converts into a real obligation to ecological stewardship.

III. Connecting with a Worldwide Crowd for Preservation

1. The Range and Variety of the Gaming People group

One of the exceptional parts of the effect of gaming on true protection is its capacity to connect with a different and worldwide crowd. The gaming local area traverses landmasses, societies, and socioeconomics, offering an exceptional chance to convey protection messages for a gigantic scope. From relaxed versatile gamers to committed esports fans, the variety inside the gaming local area considers an expansive arrive at in advancing ecological mindfulness.

2. Developing a Protection cognizant Gaming Society

As protection themed games gain notoriety, a shift happens inside the gaming society itself. Players become shoppers of diversion as well as dynamic members in a development towards natural cognizance. Gaming people group frequently coordinate occasions, gatherings, and conversations zeroed in on preservation, cultivating a feeling of shared liability and an aggregate obligation to having a constructive outcome in the world.

IV. Cooperative Associations: Game Engineers and Protection Associations

1. Utilizing Gaming Stages for Protection

Cooperation between game engineers and preservation associations has turned into a main thrust behind the effect of gaming on true protection. Game designers, perceiving their expected impact, effectively look for associations with natural gatherings to adjust virtual encounters to substantial preservation objectives. This cooperation stretches out to utilizing gaming stages as channels for spreading protection data, bringing issues to light, and empowering direct activity.

2. In-game Buys and Gifts: Gaming for a Purpose

Imaginative ways to deal with raising money inside games affect protection. In-game buys, where a piece of the returns is coordinated towards protection drives, represent a substantial manner by which the gaming business effectively adds to true causes. Players, frequently persuaded by a longing to have an effect, readily take part in these drives, adding to the monetary help of ecological associations.

V. Instructive Worth of Protection themed Games

1. Cultivating Ecological Proficiency through Ongoing interaction
   Protection themed games broaden their effect past profound commitment by filling in as instructive devices. By incorporating logical standards, natural ideas, and certifiable protection rehearses into ongoing interaction, these games encourage ecological proficiency. Players, frequently uninformed about the complexities of biological systems, wind up finding out about biodiversity, environmental change, and preservation procedures in an intelligent and drawing in way.
2. Virtual Research centers and Resident Science Drives

The instructive worth of protection themed games is additionally upgraded through the incorporation of virtual research facilities and resident science drives. Players, through their virtual encounters, effectively add to logical examination by partaking in recreated tests, information assortment, or critical thinking situations. This imaginative methodology teaches players as well as changes them into supporters of continuous logical undertakings, making a scaffold among gaming and true preservation science.

VI. Contextual investigations: Examples of overcoming adversity and Illustrations Learned

1. Games That Had an Effect
   A few preservation themed games stand apart as examples of overcoming adversity in driving certifiable effect. Games like "Eco" and "Universe of Warcraft: Disturbance" have effectively consolidated natural subjects, driving players to consider genuine environmental difficulties. The progress of these games lies in their capacity to flawlessly mix diversion with a source of inspiration, provoking players to think about their biological impression past the virtual domain.
2. Difficulties and Valuable open doors in Preservation Gaming

Nonetheless, the effect of gaming on true preservation isn't without its difficulties. Finding some kind of harmony between amusement worth and protection informing, keeping away from greenwashing, and guaranteeing long haul player commitment present continuous difficulties. Open doors for development lie in constant advancement, local area association, and addressing moral contemplations to augment the positive effect of preservation themed games.

VII. Innovative Headways and Future Possibilities

1. Vivid Advancements and Protection Encounters

   Headways in innovation, especially vivid advancements like computer generated experience (VR) and expanded reality (AR), present new roads for upgrading the effect of gaming on genuine protection. VR encounters permit players to submerge themselves in exact virtual environments, encouraging a more profound association with nature. AR applications empower players to connect with protection themed content in their actual environmental elements, making a consistent mix between the virtual and genuine universes.

2. Gamification in Ecological Schooling

Past vivid advances, the joining of gamification standards into more extensive natural instruction holds huge commitment. Gamified applications, tests, and intuitive difficulties add to a gamified way to deal with finding out about protection. By making natural schooling seriously captivating and open, gamification turns into an amazing asset in developing a culture of ecological mindfulness and obligation.

VIII. Moral Contemplations in Protection Gaming

1. Offsetting Diversion with Moral Obligation

   The effect of gaming on true protection prompts a thought of moral obligations inside the gaming business. Engineers should explore the fragile harmony between giving engaging encounters and passing on exact preservation messages. Staying away from emotionalism, guaranteeing logical exactness, and tending to potential debates become basic parts of moral game advancement in the preservation space.

2. Tending to Likely Traps and Discussions

As the impact of gaming on protection develops, likely entanglements and discussions emerge. Greenwashing, where shallow protection topics cover naturally unsafe practices inside games, requires careful investigation. Also, debates might arise encompassing the depiction of specific preservation issues or the unexpected support of hurtful generalizations. Moral contemplations request nonstop reflection and variation inside the gaming business.

IX. Difficulties and Valuable open doors: Diagramming the Course Ahead

1. Conquering Difficulties in Protection Gaming
   The excursion towards expanding the effect of gaming on genuine protection includes conquering difficulties. Adjusting to advancing player assumptions, refining preservation stories, and tending to innovative boundaries are progressing difficulties. The business should stay dexterous, open to criticism, and receptive to arising issues to guarantee that preservation themed games proceed to add to worldwide ecological objectives successfully.
2. Augmenting Potential open doors for Enduring Effect

All the while, potential open doors proliferate for augmenting the effect of gaming on genuine protection. Proceeded with advancement, cooperative organizations, and a guarantee to moral game improvement make a prolific ground for development. By boosting these open doors, the gaming business can contribute fundamentally to the continuous endeavors to address natural difficulties and motivate positive activity on a worldwide scale.

7.3 Balancing Entertainment and Responsibility

The gaming business, with its vivid and enamoring nature, faces a sensitive test: how to offset diversion esteem with moral obligation. As games become more complex and compelling, designers are progressively mindful of the need to make encounters that engage without compromising social, social, or natural qualities.

The core of adjusting amusement and obligation lies in the moral contemplations that saturate each phase of game turn of events. Designers should explore through a horde of decisions, from storyline accounts to in-game mechanics, guaranteeing that the final result lines up with moral principles and advances positive qualities.

One principal viewpoint is the depiction of assorted characters and societies. Moral game improvement includes moving past generalizations and platitudes, introducing characters that mirror the extravagance of human variety. This upgrades the gaming experience as well as adds to a more comprehensive and understanding worldwide gaming society. Games like "The Remainder of Us Part II" and "Professional killer's Belief

Valhalla" have exhibited the business' obligation to assorted and socially delicate stories.

Natural obligation is another basic thought. As virtual universes become progressively practical, designers face the moral test of portraying biological systems and untamed life precisely. Protection themed games, for example, "Eco" and "Past Blue," assume on the liability of instructing players about natural issues, cultivating a feeling of stewardship towards the planet.

In-game mechanics assume an essential part in forming player conduct. Moral contemplations here include staying away from mechanics that boost destructive activities or sustain negative generalizations. Finding some kind of harmony between drawing in ongoing interaction and mindful mechanics guarantees that players are engaged without settling on moral qualities.

Adaptation procedures additionally go under investigation. In-game buys, microtransactions, and steal from boxes can upgrade the gaming experience however ought to be carried out morally.

Straightforwardness about costs, staying away from savage practices, and guaranteeing that players are not taken advantage of add to a more capable gaming biological system.

The effect of games on psychological wellness is a developing concern, requiring capable game plan. Finding some kind of harmony between testing interactivity and staying away from habit-forming components guarantees that players can appreciate games capably without hindering consequences for their prosperity. Industry drives, similar to "Take This" and "IGDA's Down Openness Particular vested party," advocate for mindful game plan that focuses on player psychological well-being.

While handling these moral contemplations, game designers should likewise fulfill the needs of a serious market. Finding some kind of harmony between engaging ongoing interaction and moral obligation requires effective fixes. Effective games that explore this fragile harmony give pleasant encounters as well as contribute decidedly to the gaming society.

The gaming local area likewise assumes a vital part in this sensitive equilibrium. Players, outfitted with expanding mindfulness and assumptions, impact the business' direction. Vocal people group supporting for moral game turn of events and considering designers responsible add to a gaming scene that focuses on liability close by diversion.

As the gaming business advances, the significance of adjusting amusement and obligation turns out to be progressively clear. Moral game improvement isn't simply an ethical goal yet additionally an essential one.

Games that explore this equilibrium effectively reverberate with players as well as add to a positive industry notoriety.

Chapter 8

Beyond Clownfish: Exploring Other Marine Life In Gaming

The virtual expanses of gaming have for some time been an enthralling domain for players, offering a novel chance to investigate and collaborate with marine life. While clownfish have held an unmistakable spot in gaming stories, the broad prospects of virtual conditions entice the investigation of a different cluster of marine species. This investigation dives into the advancing portrayal of marine life in gaming, moving past the natural clownfish to uncover the rich embroidered artwork of the maritime world.

The Development of Marine Life Portrayal

In the beginning phases of gaming, restrictions in innovation obliged the variety of marine life portrayals. Notwithstanding, as illustrations and computational power progressed, game designers embraced the test of making sensible and different virtual biological systems. Titles like "Abzu" and "Subnautica" represent this advancement, furnishing players with vivid encounters that exhibit the perplexing excellence and assortment of marine species past the limits of clownfish-driven stories.

Variety in Virtual Biological systems

The development of gaming stories past clownfish acquaints players with a large number of marine species, from glorious whales to slippery remote ocean animals. Engineers are utilizing progressions in illustrations and man-made consciousness to make virtual biological systems that reflect the intricacy of certifiable seas. The incorporation of species variety upgrades the visual allure of games as well as adds to a more exact and instructive portrayal of marine life.

Instructive Capability of Marine Life Investigation

Past simple amusement, the investigation of different marine life in gaming holds huge instructive potential. Games become vivid home-rooms, permitting players to find out about various species, their ways of behaving, and their jobs inside environments. Instructive drives inside games, for example, intelligent field guides and enlightening pop-ups, give players an abundance of data, cultivating an appreciation for marine biodiversity and natural protection.

Challenges in Exact Portrayal

While the gaming business makes progress toward exactness in addressing marine life, challenges emerge in offsetting authenticity with the imperatives of intuitive amusement. Game designers face the sensitive assignment of keeping up with drawing in interactivity while remaining consistent with the environmental complexities of marine biological systems. Finding some kind of harmony requires coordinated effort with sea life researcher, biologists, and preservation specialists to guarantee that virtual portrayals line up with logical information.

Moral Contemplations in Marine Life Portrayal

As gaming investigates a more extensive range of marine life, moral contemplations come to the very front. Dependable game improvement includes keeping away from shady portrayals, avoiding destructive generalizations, and advancing a feeling of ecological stewardship. Engineers should explore the moral intricacies related with addressing marine life, taking into account the expected effect of player activities on virtual biological systems and true preservation perspectives.

Contextual analyses: Games Embracing Marine Variety

A few games stand apart as trailblazers in embracing the variety of marine life. "Unending Sea," for example, permits players to investigate a huge and changed submerged world, experiencing a variety of species from various maritime locales. "Apex predator" adopts a special strategy by putting players in the job of a shark, offering a point of view seldom investigated in gaming. These contextual analyses enlighten the potential outcomes and difficulties of extending the portrayal of marine life in gaming.

Mechanical Headways and Marine Life Authenticity

Progressions in innovation keep on reclassifying the authenticity of marine life portrayal in gaming. State of the art illustrations, refined liveliness, and man-made consciousness add to making exact ways of behaving and connections among virtual marine species. The incorporation of computer generated reality (VR) and increased reality (AR) advancements further improves the vivid experience, permitting players to jump into the maritime world more than ever.

Player Commitment and Preservation Effect

The consideration of different marine life in gaming improves player encounters as well as holds the possibility to drive true preservation influence. Games that underline ecological stories and protection subjects make a stage for players to interface with the significance of safeguarding marine environments.

In-game drives, for example, virtual protection activities and mindfulness crusades, enable players to add to certifiable preservation endeavors.

Investigating Underrepresented Marine Species

While famous marine species frequently become the dominant focal point in gaming accounts, there is a chance to reveal insight into underrepresented and imperiled species. Game engineers can utilize their foundation to bring issues to light about the dangers confronting species, for example, ocean turtles, seahorses, and marine vertebrates. By featuring the difficulties these species face, games can add to a more extensive discussion about preservation and the significance of safeguarding marine biodiversity.

Coordinated effort with Protection Associations

The coordinated effort between the gaming business and protection associations becomes essential in growing the portrayal of marine life. Associations can furnish engineers with significant experiences, guaranteeing that virtual portrayals line up with logical information and preservation objectives. Cooperative endeavors might reach out past game improvement to incorporate raising money drives, with a piece of game returns coordinated towards marine protection projects.

The Job of Virtual Seas in Natural Promotion

Virtual seas in gaming can possibly act as strong stages for ecological backing. Games that mesh preservation accounts into their plots, accentuating the significance of safeguarding marine life and biological systems, can move players to become advocates for ecological issues. The vivid idea of gaming considers an interesting profound association, inciting players to make an interpretation of virtual encounters into genuine protection activity.

Future Patterns in Marine Life Investigation

As innovation keeps on propelling, the investigation of marine life in gaming is ready to go through additional changes. The coordination of man-made brainpower for reasonable ways of behaving, progressions in procedural age for different biological systems, and the fuse of player-driven stories are expected future patterns. The intermingling of gaming with other arising innovations, for example, blockchain for straightforward effect following, opens new roads for ecological narrating and protection drives.

8.1 Diversity of Virtual Marine Ecosystems

The investigation of virtual marine environments in gaming has developed into a hypnotizing venture, offering players a valuable chance to jump into the profundities of different maritime universes. As innovation keeps on propelling, game engineers are bridling the force of sensible designs, modern man-made consciousness, and vivid narrating to establish virtual conditions that reflect the intricacy and magnificence of true marine environments. This investigation digs into the extensive variety of virtual marine biological systems in gaming, looking at the mechanical developments, instructive potential, and ecological effect of these intelligent maritime domains.

Mechanical Progressions Reclassifying Virtual Marine Environments

Progressions in gaming innovation assume a critical part in forming the variety of virtual marine environments. State of the art illustrations and liveliness procedures empower designers to reproduce the dynamic tones, mind boggling subtleties, and smooth motions of marine existence with phenomenal authenticity. The incorporation of man-made consciousness adds a layer of intricacy by reproducing sensible ways of behaving, cooperations, and environmental elements inside virtual seas. As players explore through these mechanically progressed conditions, they are given a vivid and genuine portrayal of the rich biodiversity tracked down in certifiable marine environments.

Procedural Age and Different Biomes

Procedural age calculations add to the variety of virtual marine biological systems by powerfully making broad and shifted biomes. Engineers utilize these calculations to produce submerged scenes, coral developments, and various marine territories that go past the impediments of physically planned conditions. The outcome is a virtual maritime world overflowing with various biological systems, each with its own remarkable greenery. This approach improves interactivity assortment as well as mirrors the natural complexities of the seas on an excellent scale.

Intelligent Biological Elements

One of the characterizing elements of virtual marine environments is the incorporation of intelligent natural elements. Not at all like static conditions, these virtual seas answer player activities, weather conditions, and biological changes. Game designers use natural displaying to recreate the interconnected connections between various species, the effect of ecological elements, and the outcomes of player choices on the general environment. This unique intuitiveness adds a layer of authenticity and intricacy, encouraging a more profound comprehension of the fragile equilibrium that supports marine life.

Instructive Capability of Virtual Marine Environments

Past amusement, virtual marine environments in gaming hold huge instructive potential. Games become vivid study halls, giving players an amazing chance to find out about sea life science, biology, and preservation in a connecting with and intuitive way. Instructive drives inside these games, for example, directed visits, enlightening pop-ups, and intuitive tests, engage players to investigate and figure out the complexities of assorted marine conditions. Via consistently coordinating instructive substance into ongoing interaction, virtual marine biological systems become an important device for cultivating natural education and mindfulness.

Different Marine Life Portrayal

The variety of virtual marine biological systems isn't just reflected in their surroundings yet in addition in the portrayal of marine life. Game engineers are progressively integrating a wide exhibit of animal groups, going from famous marine vertebrates to slippery remote ocean animals. The incorporation of different marine life goes past tasteful allure, adding to a more exact and exhaustive depiction of the seas' biodiversity. Players experience a virtual zoological display that mirrors the lavishness and assortment tracked down in various maritime locales, empowering a feeling of miracle and interest in the tremendousness of marine life.

Challenges in Exact Portrayal

While the portrayal of assorted marine environments in gaming has taken critical steps, challenges continue accomplishing precise portrayals. The constraints of momentum innovation, combined with the intricacy of marine biological systems, present difficulties in imitating each subtlety of certifiable submerged conditions. Finding some kind of harmony among authenticity and ongoing interaction requests compromises, and engineers should explore the scarce difference among precision and the requirement for connecting with intelligent encounters. Joint effort with marine specialists, researchers, and progressives becomes fundamental to guarantee that virtual portrayals line up with logical information.

Moral Contemplations in Virtual Marine Environments

As gaming investigates the variety of virtual marine environments, moral contemplations come to the front. Mindful game improvement includes keeping away from manipulative portrayals, avoiding unsafe generalizations, and advancing a feeling of natural stewardship. Designers should consider the possible effect of player activities on virtual environments and their suggestions for certifiable preservation perspectives. Moral contemplations likewise stretch out to the depiction of jeopardized species and biological systems, where responsiveness and mindfulness become urgent in encouraging a feeling of obligation among players.

Preservation Stories and Ecological Effect

Virtual marine environments frequently become the scenery for protection stories inside games. Engineers influence these accounts to impart ecological difficulties, the significance of preservation, and the results of human exercises on marine life. By meshing preservation subjects into ongoing interaction, virtual marine environments become stages for bringing issues to light and motivating players to become advocates for true protection endeavors. This natural effect goes past the virtual domain, making an extension between the gaming local area and protection drives.

Contextual analyses: Games Embracing Variety in Virtual Marine Biological systems

A few games stand apart as models in embracing the variety of virtual marine environments. "Subnautica" takes players on an outwardly shocking excursion through an outsider submerged world, exhibiting different environments and animals. "Past Blue" offers an instructive investigation of the sea, permitting players to cooperate with marine life and find out about the significance of sea protection. These contextual analyses enlighten the conceivable outcomes and difficulties of making virtual marine biological systems that enrapture players while conveying significant instructive and ecological messages.

The Job of Computer generated Reality (VR) and Increased Reality (AR)

The incorporation of computer generated reality (VR) and expanded reality (AR) advances further upgrades the variety of virtual marine environments. VR furnishes players with an unrivaled feeling of drenching, permitting them to investigate submerged conditions as though they were actually present. AR applications expand the virtual experience into this present reality, consolidating the limits between the virtual and actual conditions. These innovations raise the gaming experience as well as add to a more profound comprehension and enthusiasm for marine life.

Player Commitment and Preservation Effect

The variety of virtual marine environments improves player encounters as well as holds the possibility to drive true preservation influence. Games that stress natural stories and protection subjects make a stage for players to interface with the significance of safeguarding marine environments. In-game drives, for example, virtual preservation ventures and mindfulness crusades, enable players to add to certifiable protection endeavors. The vivid idea of gaming considers a novel profound association, inciting players to make an interpretation of virtual encounters into substantial activities that help marine protection.

Future Patterns in Virtual Marine Biological system Investigation

As innovation keeps on propelling, the investigation of virtual marine environments is ready to go through additional changes. The combination of man-made consciousness for reasonable ways of behaving, progressions in procedural age for significantly more different environments, and the consolidation of player-driven accounts are expected future patterns. The intermingling of gaming with other arising advances, for example, blockchain for straightforward effect following, opens new roads for ecological narrating and protection drives inside virtual marine biological systems.

8.2 Incorporating Various Species in Game Design

The scene of game plan has gone through a significant change, with a rising accentuation on integrating different species to make assorted and dynamic virtual universes. As innovation progresses, game engineers have extended their points of view past conventional stories, investigating the rich embroidered artwork of the normal world. This investigation dives into the importance, difficulties, and advancements related with consolidating different species in game plan, featuring the potential for vivid and instructive gaming encounters.

The Meaning of Species Variety in Game Plan

Species variety in game plan brings a huge number of advantages, improving the gaming experience and extending the story prospects. Past customary person prime examples, consolidating different species takes into consideration a more comprehensive portrayal of the normal world. Players are presented to a wide range of biological systems, each overflowing with novel vegetation, encouraging a more profound association with the extravagance of biodiversity. This approach hoists the visual allure of games as well as adds to natural instruction and mindfulness.

1. **Extending Story Skylines**

   Consolidating different species in game plan opens up new account skylines, giving engineers the amazing chance to investigate various biological systems, societies, and legends. Games like "Spore" and "No Man's Sky" represent this methodology, permitting players to explore different planets occupied by a heap of animal categories. By winding around accounts around various species, game originators can make drawing in storylines that resound with players and deal a new point of view on the interconnectedness of life.

2. **Upgrading Visual Feel**

   The visual feel of a game assume a pivotal part in drenching players in virtual universes. By consolidating different species, game planners upgrade the visual allure of conditions, presenting lively tones, perplexing subtleties, and various types of life. The juxtaposition of various species inside a virtual environment makes outwardly staggering scenes, adding to a more vivid and enrapturing gaming experience. The regard for visual feel fulfills players' tasteful inclinations as well as builds up the possibility that variety is essential to the magnificence of nature.

3. **Advancing Natural Training**

Consolidating different species in game plan fills in as an integral asset for ecological training. Games can work as intelligent study halls, offering players the potential chance to find out about various species, their ways of behaving, and their jobs inside biological systems. Instructive drives, like in-game reference books, directed visits, and educational pop-ups, furnish players with important bits of knowledge into the normal world. This combination of instruction inside interactivity cultivates a feeling of ecological proficiency and urges players to see the value in the significance of saving biodiversity.

Challenges in Consolidating Different Species

While the joining of different species brings various benefits, game originators face difficulties in accomplishing a consistent and sensible portrayal of different environments. Mechanical constraints, moral contemplations, and the requirement for adjusted ongoing interaction present obstacles that require cautious route.

1. **Mechanical Constraints**

   The sensible portrayal of different species in gaming experiences mechanical constraints, especially regarding illustrations, liveliness, and man-made consciousness. Making exact ways of behaving, perplexing environments, and reasonable connections between species requests huge computational power and refined calculations. Finding some kind of harmony between mechanical capacities and ongoing interaction requests development and consistent headways in gaming innovation.

2. **Moral Contemplations**

   Moral contemplations assume a urgent part in the joining of different species in game plan. Engineers should explore the scarcely discernible difference among diversion and mindful portrayal. Staying away from hurtful generalizations, advancing protection messages, and avoiding manipulative portrayals are fundamental parts of moral game plan. Aversion to social, environmental, and moral worries becomes fundamental to guarantee that the virtual portrayal of different species lines up with capable and comprehensive game improvement rehearses.

3. **Adjusting Authenticity and Ongoing interaction**

Accomplishing a harmony among authenticity and interactivity is a continuous test. While sensible portrayals of different species add to the vivid nature of games, they should be painstakingly incorporated into ongoing interaction to keep up with commitment. Finding some kind of harmony requires savvy fixes, creative game mechanics, and joint effort between game creators and specialists in fields like science, biology, and preservation. The test lies in making a bona fide portrayal of different species without compromising the intuitive and pleasant parts of gaming.

Developments in Consolidating Different Species

In spite of the difficulties, game originators are embracing developments to defeat mechanical and moral obstacles, pushing the limits of what is conceivable in making different and dynamic virtual universes.

1. **Procedural Age for Dynamic Environments**
   Procedural age calculations have arisen as an amazing asset for making dynamic environments with different species. These calculations produce scenes, greenery, and fauna continuously, taking into account the making of assorted and consistently changing virtual conditions. Games like "Spore" use procedural age to populate planets with a wide cluster of procedurally created species, cultivating a feeling of flightiness and extravagance in virtual environments.

2. **Man-made brainpower for Sensible Ways of behaving**
   Progressions in man-made brainpower add to the practical ways of behaving of different species in gaming. Artificial intelligence driven calculations empower virtual animals to display similar developments, social collaborations, and natural ways of behaving. This development adds a layer of intricacy to virtual environments, making a more real and vivid experience for players. Games like "Red Dead Recovery 2" feature the capability of computer based intelligence driven natural life conduct, where different species connect with one another and answer the player's activities.

3. **Expanded Reality (AR) for Certifiable Joining**

The coordination of increased reality (AR) takes into consideration the overlay of virtual species onto this present reality, overcoming any barrier between the virtual and actual conditions. AR applications, for example, "Pokemon Go," show the way that different species can be consistently incorporated into players' environmental factors. This development expands the gaming experience past the screen, furnishing players with a clever method for communicating with virtual species in their ordinary surroundings.

Instructive Drives inside Interactivity

Game creators are integrating instructive drives inside ongoing interaction to upgrade's comprehension players might interpret different species and their natural importance. Intelligent field guides, useful pop-ups, and in-game difficulties that require information about various species add to the instructive benefit of gaming. Via flawlessly incorporating instructive substance into interactivity, planners enable players to investigate, learn, and value the variety of species inside virtual universes.

Contextual analyses: Games Succeeding in Species Variety

A few games stand apart as trailblazers in succeeding at species variety in game plan. "Planet Zoo" permits players to make and deal with their own zoo, including a different scope of animal varieties from different natural surroundings. "ABZÛ" takes players on a submerged excursion, experiencing an assortment of marine life. These contextual analyses feature how the joining of different species improves interactivity and adds to the general progress of the gaming experience.

Player Commitment and Ecological Effect

The joining of different species in game plan not just draws in players on a visual and story level yet additionally holds the possibility to drive ecological effect. Games that underline protection subjects and grandstand the significance of biodiversity can rouse players to become advocates for genuine ecological endeavors. In-game drives, for example, virtual preservation undertakings and mindfulness crusades, enable players to add to unmistakable protection activities, overcoming any barrier among virtual and genuine effect.

Future Patterns in Species Variety in Game Plan

The eventual fate of game plan is ready to observe further headways in species variety, driven by mechanical developments and a developing accentuation on ecological cognizance. Arising patterns incorporate the reconciliation of blockchain for straightforward effect following, cooperative undertakings between game designers and protection associations, and the usage of computer generated reality (VR) to make significantly more vivid and instructive encounters.

8.3 Future Possibilities and Innovations

The scene of game plan is a dynamic and consistently developing domain, driven by mechanical headways, imaginative investigation, and the advancing assumptions for players. As we look towards the future, a large number of conceivable outcomes and developments arise, promising to rethink the gaming experience. This investigation digs into the astonishing possibilities and developments that could shape the fate of game plan, from state of the art advances to novel narrating approaches.

1. Computer generated Reality (VR) and Vivid Encounters
   Computer generated Reality (VR) remains at the front of changing the gaming experience into a genuinely vivid excursion. As VR innovation keeps on propelling, future games are ready to offer

uncommon degrees of drenching, permitting players to step into virtual universes with an increased feeling of presence. VR headsets, haptic criticism frameworks, and movement detecting regulators add to making a multisensory experience that rises above conventional gaming limits.

The potential for VR stretches out past visual and hear-able boosts, integrating contact, development, and, surprisingly, olfactory sensations to establish a really all encompassing gaming climate. Future games could use VR to move players into fantastical domains, authentic settings, or even the tiny world, giving an unmatched feeling of investigation and presence.

2. **Increased Reality (AR) Incorporation into Day to day existence**
   Increased Reality (AR) can possibly overcome any issues among virtual and certifiable encounters, consistently coordinating interactivity into the texture of daily existence. As AR innovation develops, games could unfurl in true conditions, with virtual components existing together with actual environmental elements. This reconciliation could appear as area based games, instructive encounters, or intelligent stories that unfurl in the player's prompt environmental elements.

   Envision a game where players set out on a journey that drives them to verifiable milestones, parks, and social centers, with AR upgrading their impression of this present reality by overlaying intelligent components and storylines. This union of virtual and true components could rethink how players draw in with games, transforming the whole world into a material for intelligent narrating.

3. **Blockchain Innovation for Straightforward Gaming Biological systems**
   Blockchain innovation can possibly reform the gaming business by presenting straightforwardness, possession, and decentralized environments. Later on, blockchain could be used for secure and straightforward thing possession, empowering players to really claim and exchange game resources across various games or stages. This could prompt the development of player-driven economies where virtual resources hold true worth.

   Shrewd agreements on blockchain could likewise work with player-driven administration, permitting networks to have something to do with the turn of events and bearing of their number one games. The decentralized idea of blockchain could relieve issues like misrepresentation, cheating, and unjustifiable works on, making a more impartial and player-driven gaming climate.

4. Man-made brainpower (simulated intelligence) and Dynamic Narrating

The combination of Computerized reasoning (simulated intelligence) into game plan holds the commitment of dynamic and versatile narrating. Future games could highlight simulated intelligence driven stories that answer player decisions, feelings, and playstyles, making a customized and developing gaming experience. Simulated intelligence calculations could examine player conduct continuously, changing the account, difficulties, and even characters in light of individual inclinations.

This dynamic narrating approach could prompt games with practically vast conceivable outcomes, where each playthrough offers a novel and custom fitted experience. Simulated intelligence associates inside games could advance in light of player collaborations, creating characters and connections that reflect the intricacy of human associations.

5. Procedural Age for Limitless Universes

Procedural age, currently used in games like "Minecraft" and "No Man's Sky," is ready to advance further, offering the potential for really endless and various virtual universes. High level procedural calculations could produce scenes as well as mind boggling biological systems, urban areas, and societies inside games. This would prompt far reaching and dynamic game universes that vibe alive, continually advancing and answering player activities.

Future games could use procedural age to make reasonable and various environments, where greenery collaborate with one another in complex ways. This wouldn't just upgrade the visual allure of games yet in addition add to a more vivid and capricious gaming experience.

6. Neurogaming and Cerebrum PC Points of interaction

Neurogaming, the convergence of neuroscience and gaming, holds the commitment of direct correspondence between the cerebrum and virtual conditions. Cerebrum PC interfaces (BCIs) could empower players to control in-game activities, explore menus, or even experience feelings inside the game straightforwardly through their brain signals. This degree of direct collaboration can possibly rethink how players draw in with and experience games.

Envision a game where a player's feelings impact the story, or where tackling puzzles requires mental concentration and critical thinking abilities. Neurogaming could open up new roads for openness, permitting people with actual handicaps to draw in with games in original ways, making a more comprehensive gaming scene.

7. **Maintainability and Eco-Accommodating Game Turn of events**
The eventual fate of game plan is probably going to see an expanded accentuation on manageability and eco-accommodating practices. As the gaming business wrestles with its natural effect, designers might embrace eco-cognizant methodologies, from energy-proficient game motors to maintainable bundling and dependable asset the board.
Games themselves could incorporate natural subjects, cultivating mindfulness and empowering players to think about true protection and supportability endeavors. This could prompt a change in perspective where game improvement turns into a main impetus for positive ecological change, lining up with more extensive worldwide endeavors towards supportability.

8. **Cross-Stage and Cross-Reality Incorporation**

The eventual fate of gaming is probably going to see consistent coordination across stages and real factors. Cross-stage gaming, where players can consistently switch between control center, laptops, and cell phones, is now turning out to be more normal. The subsequent stage includes the coordination of various real factors, where players can progress between virtual, increased, and actual conditions.

Envision a game where players start a mission in a virtual world utilizing VR, proceed with the experience in an expanded reality (AR) setting as they stroll through a recreation area, and afterward get in-game rewards that can be utilized in the actual world. This interconnected and liquid experience could rethink the limits of conventional gaming and make a more all encompassing type of intuitive diversion.

Chapter 9

The Intersection Of Science And Gaming

The domain where science and gaming cross addresses an interesting outskirts where development, schooling, and diversion combine. As innovation keeps on propelling, game designers progressively draw motivation from logical standards, adding to a cooperative relationship that benefits the two fields. This investigation dives into the multi-layered crossing point of science and gaming, inspecting how logical ideas impact game plan, the instructive capability of games, and the cooperative endeavors among researchers and engineers.

1. Logical Ideas in Game Plan

   The coordination of logical ideas into game plan addresses a dynamic and developing pattern that improves the genuineness and intricacy of virtual universes. Game engineers draw motivation from different logical disciplines, including material science, science, stargazing, and that's only the tip of the iceberg, to make vivid and reasonable gaming encounters.

   1.1 Physical science Reenactments and Sensible Mechanics

   Physical science reenactments assume a critical part in present day game plan, adding to sensible mechanics, liquid movements, and exact communications inside virtual conditions. Game motors influence standards of physical science to reenact gravity, movement, and impacts, making a feeling of realness that improves player drenching. Titles like "Fantastic Burglary Auto V" and "Kerbal Space Program" feature the use of physical science based reproductions, permitting players to encounter practical vehicle elements and orbital mechanics.

   1.2 Natural Frameworks and Environment in Gaming

   Natural frameworks and environmental standards track down

articulation in gaming through the reenactment of biological systems, development, and creature ways of behaving. Games like "Spore" and "Planet Zoo" influence natural ideas to make dynamic and developing virtual universes. Players cooperate with biological systems, notice the ways of behaving of virtual animals, and witness the outcomes of ecological changes, giving an instructive encounter that reflects the intricacies of the regular world.

1.3 Galactic Precision in Space Investigation Games

Space investigation games frequently take a stab at galactic precision, consolidating genuine divine bodies, orbital mechanics, and infinite peculiarities. Titles like "World class Perilous" and "Kerbal Space Program" reenact the immensity of room, offering players the chance to explore star frameworks, experience gravitational powers, and participate in interplanetary travel. This obligation to logical exactness enhances the gaming experience as well as encourages an appreciation for the miracles of the universe.

1.4 Science Riddles and Speculative chemistry in Ongoing interaction

Science ideas manifest in gaming through puzzles, creating frameworks, and catalytic mechanics. Games like "The Observer" integrate science based puzzles that require a comprehension of atomic designs and holding standards. Moreover, dream games frequently highlight speculative chemistry frameworks where players join virtual fixings to make elixirs or enchanted substances, drawing motivation from true synthetic responses.

2. Instructive Capability of Science-Based Games

The convergence of science and gaming reaches out past simple diversion, offering a strong stage for instruction. Science-based games can possibly connect with players in intuitive growth opportunities, making complex ideas available and agreeable. Instructive games range different disciplines, giving open doors to players to investigate, explore, and foster a more profound comprehension of logical standards.

2.1 Gamified Learning Conditions

Gamified learning conditions influence the intuitive and persuasive parts of gaming to work with schooling. Stages like "Minecraft: Training Version" integrate instructive modules that cover themes going from arithmetic to history. These conditions empower investigation and innovativeness, encouraging a vivid instructive encounter where understudies effectively draw in with topic through interactivity.

2.2 Recreation Games for STEM Instruction

Recreation games assume a vital part in STEM (Science, Innovation,

Designing, and Math) training, permitting understudies to apply hypothetical information in down to earth settings. Titles, for example, "Urban communities: Horizons" and "Factorio" recreate metropolitan preparation and designing difficulties, giving experiences into complex frameworks. These games offer an involved way to deal with picking up, empowering understudies to try different things with ideas and notice the outcomes of their choices.

2.3 Resident Science and Cooperative Gaming

Resident science drives tackle the aggregate force of gamers to add to true logical exploration. Games like "Foldit" welcome players to address complex protein-collapsing puzzles, contributing important bits of knowledge to logical investigations. Cooperative gaming projects empower players to effectively partake in logical undertakings, overcoming any barrier between gaming networks and mainstream researchers.

2.4 Virtual Research facilities and Trials

Virtual research facilities inside instructive games recreate tests, permitting understudies to investigate logical ideas in a protected and controlled climate. Games like "Labster" and "PhET Intelligent Recreations" offer virtual labs covering material science, science, science, and the sky is the limit from there. These reenactments give understudies potential chances to lead tests, mention objective facts, and support hypothetical information through active encounters.

3. ## Cooperative Endeavors among Researchers and Game Designers

   The coordinated effort among researchers and game engineers has become progressively predominant, prompting the formation of games that engage as well as add to logical exploration and public comprehension of logical ideas.

3.1 Game Designers as Science Communicators

Game designers act as science communicators, making an interpretation of intricate logical ideas into connecting with and available gaming encounters. Titles like "Never Alone" consolidate native social accounts, giving players experiences into conventional information and encouraging social appreciation. Game designers add to science correspondence by making logical data engaging and convincing to different crowds.

3.2 Serious Games for Wellbeing and Medication

Serious games planned in a joint effort with medical services experts add to clinical schooling, preparing, and treatment. Games like "Visualization: Your Determination" and "Careful Test system" furnish clinical understudies and experts with sensible situations for ability advancement and indicative preparation. These serious games upgrade clinical schooling by offering intelligent and commonsense growth opportunities.

3.3 Information Assortment through Gaming

Resident science projects installed inside games work with information assortment for logical examination. Games like "EteRNA" and "EyeWire" connect with players in addressing puzzles connected with RNA collapsing and brain planning. The information created by players add to progressing logical investigations, showing the capability of gaming networks to make significant commitments to logical exploration.

3.4 Computer generated Simulation for Logical Investigation

Computer generated reality (VR) advances empower researchers to investigate and picture information in vivid ways. Coordinated efforts among researchers and VR engineers bring about applications that permit analysts to explore complex datasets, picture sub-atomic designs, and reenact logical peculiarities. VR improves logical investigation by giving new points of view and intuitive instruments for information examination.

4. Moral Contemplations in Science-Based Gaming

The crossing point of science and gaming raises moral contemplations connected with precise portrayal, capable gamification of learning, and the likely effect on player view of logical ideas.

4.1 Precision and Portrayal

Guaranteeing precision in the portrayal of logical ideas is vital to keeping up with the instructive worth of science-based games. Designers should figure out some kind of harmony among amusement and constancy to logical standards, trying not to misdirect depictions that could propagate misguided judgments. Cooperative endeavors among researchers and designers become fundamental to maintain the uprightness of instructive substance.

4.2 Gamification of Learning and Inspiration

The gamification of learning, while successful in connecting with understudies, requires cautious thought of moral ramifications. Adjusting the inspirational parts of gaming with instructive objectives requires careful plan to forestall shallow commitment. Moral contemplations incorporate keeping away from the double-dealing of extraneous rewards and guaranteeing that instructive substance stays the essential focal point of the gaming experience.

4.3 Variety and Inclusivity in Science Portrayal

Science-based games ought to take a stab at variety and inclusivity in the portrayal of researchers, specialists, and logical stories. Addressing generalizations and predispositions in game plan adds to a more comprehensive and precise depiction of mainstream researchers. Moral contemplations reach out to social awareness, perceiving and regarding different points of view inside the gaming crowd.

4.4 Informed Assent in Resident Science Games

Games that include resident science and information assortment should focus on informed assent and moral information rehearses. Players adding to logical exploration through gaming ought to be completely educated about the reason regarding information assortment, how their commitments will be utilized, and the ramifications of their association. Moral rules guarantee that players partake deliberately and with an unmistakable comprehension of the cooperative idea of these drives.

5. The Eventual fate of Science and Gaming Joint effort

As the crossing point of science and gaming keeps on advancing, what's to come holds energizing opportunities for additional coordinated effort, development, and effect.

5.1 Progressions in Computer generated Experience and Expanded Reality

Headways in computer generated experience (VR) and expanded reality (AR) advancements will probably open new boondocks for logical investigation and training. VR reenactments could offer specialists vivid encounters to envision complex information, while AR applications could give intuitive overlays to true logical perceptions. The assembly of these advances holds the possibility to alter how researchers lead examination and offer their discoveries with the general population.

5.2 Proceeded with Development of Resident Science Gaming

The development of resident science gaming is ready to proceed, with additional games incorporating player commitments into logical exploration. Cooperative ventures between gaming networks and logical organizations might grow to cover a more extensive scope of disciplines, outfitting the aggregate force of players to address true difficulties. This comprehensive way to deal with exploration could rethink the connection among researchers and general society.

5.3 Gamified Answers for Worldwide Difficulties

Games intended to address worldwide difficulties, for example, environmental change, general wellbeing, and maintainability, may turn out to be more common. Coordinated efforts between researchers, policymakers, and game designers could result in gamified arrangements that connect with players in understanding and resolving major problems.

These games can possibly prepare aggregate activity and bring issues to light on a worldwide scale.

5.4 Joining of man-made intelligence and AI in Science-Based Games

The joining of man-made reasoning (computer based intelligence) and AI in science-based games could prompt dynamic and responsive gaming encounters.

Artificial intelligence calculations might adjust instructive substance in view of individual player progress, giving customized learning ways. Also, AI models could improve the authenticity of reproductions by creating more perplexing and similar virtual conditions.

9.1 Collaborations between Marine Biologists and Game Developers

The joint effort between sea life scientists and game engineers addresses an extraordinary and productive convergence of science and innovation. As how we might interpret the seas grows, so does the potential for utilizing virtual conditions to teach, bring issues to light, and add to marine protection endeavors. This investigation digs into the different joint efforts between sea life researcher and game engineers, looking at the development of marine-themed games, the instructive effect of virtual sea investigation, and the job of these coordinated efforts in propelling sea life science and protection.

1. Development of Marine-Themed Games

   The marriage of sea life science and game improvement has brought about an astonishing type of games that submerge players in the miracles of the sea. From the beginning of pixelated marine animals to the modern reproductions of today, marine-themed games have advanced in both intricacy and instructive worth.

   1.1 Spearheading Marine Investigation in Games

   The excursion starts with early titles like "Ecco the Dolphin" and "Unending Sea," which acquainted players with submerged universes populated by an assortment of marine life. These games, while principally centered around amusement, established the groundwork for future coordinated efforts by catching the creative mind of players and encouraging an appreciation for the secrets of the sea.

   1.2 Authenticity and Logical Exactness

   As innovation progressed, game engineers looked to upgrade the authenticity and logical precision of marine-themed games. Titles like "Abzu" and "Past Blue" grandstand outwardly staggering submerged conditions, reasonable marine ways of behaving, and a guarantee to depicting the magnificence and delicacy of sea environments. This shift towards exactness lines up with the cooperative endeavors between sea life scientists and game designers to guarantee that virtual portrayals reflect the intricacies of certifiable marine conditions.

1.3 Instructive and Preservation centered Games

Ongoing years have seen the development of instructive and protection centered games that influence the skill of sea life scholars. Games, for example, "Never Alone: Cold Assortment" and "Past Blue" integrate stories roused by sea life science, offering players an instructive excursion through the eyes of researchers and specialists. These games engage as well as act as amazing assets for bringing issues to light about marine protection challenges.

2. **Instructive Effect of Virtual Sea Investigation**

The joint effort between sea life scientists and game engineers reaches out past diversion, opening the potential for virtual sea investigation to turn into an extraordinary instructive device. Through painstakingly made games, players can leave on instructive excursions, acquiring bits of knowledge into sea life science, biology, and preservation.

2.1 Vivid Learning Conditions

Virtual sea investigation games give vivid learning conditions where players can interface with marine life, investigate submerged environments, and find the interconnectedness of species. Titles like "Past Blue" utilize computer generated reality (VR) to make a much more vivid experience, permitting players to feel like they are essential for a marine examination endeavor.

2.2 Gamified Learning Modules

Instructive games frequently integrate gamified learning modules that mix amusement with logical information. These modules cover a scope of subjects, from marine species distinguishing proof to the effect of environmental change on sea biological systems. The gamification of learning makes complex logical ideas open and drawing in, engaging an expansive crowd, including understudies, teachers, and long lasting students.

2.3 Resident Science Drives

Cooperative undertakings between sea life scholars and game engineers stretch out past the computerized domain to incorporate resident science drives. Games like "Fishackathon" and "Ocean Legend Journey" influence player commitments to gather important information for logical exploration. By transforming ongoing interaction into a type of resident science, these joint efforts enable players to effectively partake in marine exploration, adding to how we might interpret the seas.

3. **Propelling Sea life Science and Protection**

The coordinated efforts between sea life scholars and game engineers assume an essential part in propelling sea life science and protection endeavors. These organizations add to logical exploration, bring issues to light about marine issues, and move another age of sea advocates.

3.1 Information Assortment and Examination

Games planned in a joint effort with sea life scientists frequently consolidate information assortment systems inside the ongoing interaction. Players, through their virtual investigations, contribute important information that scientists can examine to acquire experiences into marine biological systems. This imaginative way to deal with information assortment broadens the span of sea life science, utilizing the aggregate endeavors of gamers to improve how we might interpret the seas.

3.2 Bringing issues to light and Protection Informing

The story driven approach of numerous marine-themed games fills in as an integral asset for bringing issues to light about marine protection challenges. Games frequently integrate protection informing, resolving issues, for example, overfishing, plastic contamination, and environmental change. By submerging players in these virtual situations, game designers and sea life researcher expect to summon compassion and a feeling of obligation towards the seas.

3.3 Empowering Economical Practices

Coordinated efforts between sea life scholars and game designers add to the advancement of supportable practices in the gaming business. By featuring natural issues inside the story of games, these coordinated efforts urge players to think about this present reality effect of their activities. This expanding influence reaches out past the virtual domain, cultivating a feeling of ecological obligation among the gaming local area.

3.4 Rousing Future Sea life Researchers

Instructive games that grandstand the energy and difficulties of sea life science can possibly rouse people in the future of sea life researchers. By giving a virtual stage to hopeful specialists to investigate marine conditions and participate in logical exercises, these joint efforts add to the development of a different and enthusiastic local area of people focused on the review and protection of the seas.

4. Difficulties and Contemplations

While coordinated efforts between sea life scholars and game engineers hold incredible commitment, they likewise face difficulties and moral contemplations.

Finding some kind of harmony between diversion, precision, and mindful portrayal is urgent to guarantee that these coordinated efforts accomplish their instructive and preservation objectives.

4.1 Precision and Logical Respectability

Keeping up with logical exactness and honesty inside games is quite difficult for joint efforts between sea life scholars and game designers. Finding some kind of harmony among authenticity and amusement frequently includes rearrangements or creative freedoms, bringing up issues about how precisely virtual portrayals mirror the intricacies of marine biological systems. Straightforward correspondence among researchers and designers is fundamental to guarantee that the instructive substance remains logically sound.

4.2 Moral Portrayal of Marine Life

Moral contemplations encompass the portrayal of marine life inside games. Games should try not to sustain unsafe generalizations, ridiculous ways of behaving, or shifty portrayals of marine species. Joint efforts ought to focus on moral portrayal, considering the biological significance and preservation status of species highlighted in virtual conditions.

4.3 Inclusivity and Social Responsiveness

Inclusivity and social awareness are contemplations that reach out past logical precision. Coordinated efforts ought to endeavor to address assorted points of view, societies, and native information connected with the seas. Recognizing the worldwide idea of sea life science and protection encourages a more comprehensive and socially delicate way to deal with virtual sea investigation.

4.4 Adjusting Preservation Informing and Diversion

The harmony between preservation informing and diversion esteem is a sensitive thought. While bringing issues to light about marine preservation challenges is urgent, games should abstain from turning out to be excessively instructive or forfeiting interactivity pleasure. Finding some kind of harmony guarantees that players stay connected with, responsive to protection messages, and inspired to make true moves.

5. Future Headings and Developments

As joint efforts between sea life scientists and game engineers keep on advancing, future headings and advancements hold the possibility to extend the effect of virtual sea investigation on training, exploration, and protection.

5.1 Joining of Arising Innovations

The combination of arising advancements, like expanded reality (AR) and computer generated reality (VR), is probably going to assume a huge part in store for marine-themed games. These advances offer new elements of drenching, permitting players to encounter submerged conditions in manners that intently mirror genuine circumstances. VR, specifically, gives an open door to a more genuine and instinctive investigation of the seas.

5.2 Proceeded with Resident Science Commitment

The idea of resident science inside games is supposed to develop, with a rising number of cooperative undertakings drawing in players in true information assortment. Proceeded with endeavors to configuration games that work with significant commitments to logical examination engage players to become dynamic members in sea life science tries. This cooperative methodology grows the scope of exploration as well as reinforces the association among gamers and established researchers.

5.3 Worldwide Coordinated efforts for Sea Promotion

Coordinated efforts between sea life scholars and game engineers can possibly develop into worldwide drives for sea backing. Connecting with players overall in a common virtual investigation of the seas encourages a feeling of worldwide obligation regarding marine protection. Game engineers, researchers, and players can by and large add to tending to squeezing sea issues on a worldwide scale.

5.4 Interdisciplinary Associations

Future coordinated efforts might observer an expansion in interdisciplinary associations that reach out past sea life science and game turn of events. Including specialists from fields like ecological brain research, instructive innovation, and human-PC cooperation could prompt imaginative methodologies in planning games that boost instructive effect, commitment, and social change.

9.2Educational Potential for Science Communication

Science correspondence assumes a critical part in making an interpretation of mind boggling logical ideas into open and connecting with stories for people in general. In the contemporary period, where data is plentiful yet frequently overpowering, viable science correspondence fills in as an extension between established researchers and the more extensive public. This investigation digs into the instructive potential intrinsic in science correspondence, looking at its job in advancing logical education, cultivating public commitment, and motivating an oddity driven way to deal with learning.

1. The Substance of Science Correspondence

   Science correspondence is a complicated course of passing logical information on to different crowds in a manner that is understandable, engaging, and convincing. At its center, science correspondence looks to separate the obstructions that might exist between established researchers and the overall population, cultivating a two-way exchange that enhances grasping on the two closures.

1.1 Discussing Intricacy with Clearness

One of the essential difficulties in science correspondence lies in refining multifaceted logical ideas into language and visuals that resound with non-specialists. Whether it includes making sense of the intricacies of quantum physical science or unwinding the complexities of environmental change, viable science correspondence endeavors to make data available without distorting or compromising precision.

1.2 Narrating as a Useful asset

Narrating arises as a useful asset in science correspondence, winding around stories that charm crowds and work with a more profound association with logical substance. By integrating components of narrating, communicators can change unique thoughts into interesting stories, making science a group of information as well as a convincing story that unfurls through revelation, challenge, and win.

1.3 Multi-Modular Ways to deal with Commitment

Perceiving the variety in learning inclinations, science correspondence embraces multi-modular methodologies that go past conventional composed designs. Webcasts, recordings, infographics, intuitive sites, and virtual entertainment stages become dynamic materials for passing on logical data. These methodologies upgrade commitment by taking special care of shifted learning styles and inclinations, guaranteeing that logical substance contacts crowds through channels they see as generally available.

2. Advancing Logical Proficiency

At its center, the instructive capability of science correspondence lies in advancing logical proficiency — a major comprehension of logical ideas and the logical strategy. Logical proficiency enables people to fundamentally assess data, settle on informed choices, and effectively partake in conversations on logical subjects.

2.1 Supporting Interest and Request

Compelling science correspondence has the ability to light and sustain interest, moving people to get clarification on pressing issues, look for replies, and move toward the world with a curious attitude.

By exhibiting the marvel of logical revelation and the excitement of disentangling secrets, science communicators support the improvement of an oddity driven way to deal with learning.

2.2 Tending to Confusions and Legends

Logical education includes dissipating misguided judgments and legends that might course in the public area. Science correspondence goes about as a restorative power, giving precise data to counter deception and cultivating a culture of reality checking. By tending to confusions head-on, communicators add to a more educated and logically proficient society.

2.3 Interfacing Science to Regular daily existence

Making science pertinent to regular daily existence is a vital part of advancing logical education. Science correspondence tries to outline the reasonable uses of logical standards in regions like wellbeing, innovation, and the climate. By showing how science converges with everyday encounters, communicators overcome any barrier between theoretical ideas and unmistakable, certifiable pertinence.

3. Encouraging Public Commitment and Cooperation

Instruction through science correspondence stretches out past the securing of information; it supports dynamic investment and commitment with logical thoughts. Public commitment turns into a powerful trade where people consume data as well as add to conversations, share points of view, and team up on resident science drives.

3.1 Resident Science and Cooperative Ventures

Science correspondence stages frequently consolidate resident science projects, welcoming the general population to add to logical examination effectively. Drives like bird counting, plant perception, or cosmic system grouping influence the aggregate force of resident researchers, transforming general society into important teammates in the logical cycle. By cultivating a feeling of interest, science correspondence enables people to contribute seriously to progressing research endeavors.

3.2 Exchanges and back and forth Discussions

Intelligent components, for example, live interactive discussions and public gatherings, make spaces for direct commitment among researchers and general society. These discoursed permit people to offer conversation starters, look for explanations, and participate in conversations with specialists. The openness of these communications improves public comprehension and demystifies established researchers, encouraging a feeling of shared interest and disclosure.

3.3 Virtual Labs and Reenactments

Progressions in innovation empower the making of virtual labs and recreations, giving the public active, intuitive encounters. Science correspondence use these devices to recreate logical tests, permitting people to investigate ideas going from science to physical science in a virtual climate. This vivid methodology improves commitment by changing detached learning into dynamic investigation.

4. Science Correspondence in Conventional Schooling

The instructive capability of science correspondence reaches out to formal instructive settings, enhancing homeroom encounters and supporting conventional educating techniques. Incorporating science correspondence into formal training lines up with the more extensive objective of developing a deductively educated society.

4.1 Upgrading Study hall Learning

Science correspondence supplements customary study hall advancing by offering valuable materials, media assets, and intuitive substance. Teachers can use science correspondence stages to improve illustrations, give genuine setting, and flash interest in logical subjects. This reconciliation encourages a dynamic and drawing in learning climate.

4.2 Spanning Holes in Admittance to Schooling

Science correspondence has the ability to connect holes in admittance to training by giving free, online assets that contact worldwide crowds. Online stages, instructive recordings, and intelligent sites guarantee that people, paying little mind to geological area or financial status, can get to excellent logical substance. This democratization of data adds to a more comprehensive and fair way to deal with instruction.

4.3 Expert Improvement for Teachers

Science correspondence offers amazing open doors for proficient advancement among instructors. Studios, online courses, and assets furnished by science communicators enable instructors with compelling correspondence techniques, inventive showing draws near, and the most recent logical updates. This cooperative connection between science communicators and instructors improves the general nature of science training.

5. Moral Contemplations in Science Correspondence

As science correspondence expects a focal job in forming public discernments and perspectives towards science, moral contemplations become fundamental. Finding some kind of harmony between availability, exactness, and dependable portrayal is fundamental to maintain the respectability of science correspondence endeavors.

5.1 Exactness and Straightforwardness

Keeping up with exactness in logical correspondence is a primary moral rule. Communicators should endeavor to introduce data honestly, recognizing vulnerabilities when appropriate. Straightforwardness about the logical interaction, including the constraints of examination and possible areas of dispute, fabricates entrust with the crowd and advances a nuanced comprehension of logical information.

5.2 Staying away from Sentimentality and Distortion

Moral science correspondence abstains from emotionalism or deception of logical discoveries. While the appeal of exciting titles might stand out, it chances misshaping the logical story and advancing deception. Dependable communicators focus on precision over sentimentality, guaranteeing that general society gets a nuanced and proof based depiction of logical revelations.

5.3 Social Awareness and Inclusivity

Science correspondence ought to be socially delicate and comprehensive, perceiving the different foundations and viewpoints of its crowd. Communicators ought to abstain from building up generalizations or coincidentally barring specific networks. Embracing social variety guarantees that logical stories reverberate with an expansive crowd and encourages a comprehensive academic local area.

5.4 Tending to Disputable Points with Care

Questionable logical themes request cautious and sympathetic correspondence. Moral science correspondence includes recognizing contrasting perspectives, introducing proof fair-mindedly, and encouraging aware discourse. By moving toward questionable subjects with care, communicators can make a space for informed conversation and decisive reasoning without polarizing crowds.

6. Utilizing Innovation for Upgraded Correspondence

Headways in innovation offer science communicators a plenty of devices to improve instructive effort. From computer generated reality encounters to intuitive internet based stages, innovation fills in as an impetus for creative and drawing in science correspondence.

6.1 Computer generated Simulation and Increased Reality Encounters

Computer generated reality (VR) and increased reality (AR) advances give vivid encounters that transport crowds into logical domains. Virtual field trips, intelligent recreations, and AR-improved displays rejuvenate science, offering people the valuable chance to investigate conditions that may somehow be out of reach.

These advances intensify the instructive effect of science correspondence by making vital and groundbreaking encounters.

6.2 Intuitive Sites and Applications

The improvement of intuitive sites and versatile applications changes detached utilization of data into dynamic commitment. Science correspondence stages can consolidate tests, games, and intuitive components that support learning and make the instructive experience more pleasant. Intelligent elements take care of assorted learning styles and improve information maintenance.

6.3 Web-based Entertainment and Science Powerhouses

Web-based entertainment stages act as integral assets for science correspondence, permitting communicators to contact huge crowds and start discussions. Science powerhouses, who mix skill with appealing correspondence styles, influence stages like Instagram, Twitter, and YouTube to scatter logical data. These powerhouses make online networks where people can draw in with science in an available and casual way.

6.4 Internet based Courses and Online classes

The ascent of online schooling stages empowers science communicators to propose inside and out courses, online courses, and studios. These assets furnish people with the chance to dig into explicit logical points, clarify pressing issues, and interface with specialists. Internet learning stages add to the democratization of instruction by making particular logical information more available.

7. Future Headings: Extending Skylines in Science Correspondence

As science correspondence keeps on developing, future headings point towards growing skylines, embracing new innovations, and cultivating a worldwide local area that qualities and figures out the significance of logical information.

7.1 Worldwide Joint efforts for Science Correspondence

Worldwide joint efforts between science communicators, teachers, and specialists can possibly intensify the effect of science correspondence endeavors. By sharing assets, mastery, and social bits of knowledge, communicators can make content that resounds with different crowds around the world. Cooperative drives could rise above geological limits, adding to a more interconnected and informed worldwide local area.

7.2 Consolidating Assorted Points of view

Future science correspondence endeavors ought to effectively search out and integrate assorted points of view. Embracing voices from various societies, foundations, and networks enhances the stories introduced in science correspondence.

Stages ought to endeavor to be comprehensive, guaranteeing that an expansive scope of voices is heard and that logical substance is important and engaging to different crowds.

7.3 Versatile Learning Innovations

Progressions in versatile learning advances hold guarantee for fitting science correspondence encounters to individual learning styles and inclinations. Versatile stages can investigate client connections and convey customized content, guaranteeing that instructive encounters are drawing in, compelling, and take special care of the one of a kind requirements of every student.

7.4 Assessing Effect and Viability

The fate of science correspondence includes a coordinated work to evaluate the effect and viability of correspondence procedures. Evaluative measures, like reviews, criticism instruments, and information investigation, can give bits of knowledge into how well science correspondence is accomplishing its instructive objectives. Nonstop evaluation permits communicators to refine their methodologies and amplify the positive results of their endeavors.

9.3Inspiring a New Generation of Marine Biologists and Game Designers

Motivating another age of sea life scientists and game architects requires the combination of science and innovativeness. By submerging hopeful personalities in the enthralling universe of virtual seas, where marine life wakes up through intuitive gaming encounters, we develop an enthusiasm for sea life science and game plan. These undertakings not just flash interest in the secrets of the submerged domain yet additionally impart a feeling of obligation towards sea preservation. Through inventive and instructive interactivity, we support the following rush of experts who will investigate, comprehend, and safeguard the seas, crossing over the domains of sea life science and advanced imagination.